Everything You Didn't Need to Know About The

Printed and bound in Great Britain by Butler & Tanner Ltd, Frome, Somerset

Published by Sanctuary Publishing Limited, Sanctuary House,
45–53 Sinclair Road, London W14 0NS, United Kingdom

www.sanctuarypublishing.com

Copyright: © Sanctuary Publishing Limited, 2003

Cover concept: Splashdown
Cover illustration: Peter Quinnell
Illustrations: Axos

ISBN: 1-86074-556-3

Everything You Didn't Need to Know About The

Karen Farrington

Sanctuary

ACKNOWLEDGEMENTS

Grateful thanks to Teresa Councell, Mark Asher and Nick Constable, for without them the book would remain incomplete.

PREFACE

Everyone knows something about the United States of America. It's impossible to get far into adulthood without gleaning some snippets about 'The Big Country' from Hollywood films, corporate advertising, news broadcasts, nature programmes or even *The Guiness Book Of World Records*.

This book is designed to give you more information about America than you ever had before. It will prove, if proof were needed, that stateside there are literally scores of things you never knew you never knew.

Why? Well, it's impossible to wring out the essence of America and pop it in a package for sale and consumption. This is more continent than country. It has a thousand or more different identities and, just when you think you're getting to the beating heart of America, you learn something new that creates more questions than answers.

It's surely a mistake to embrace everything American without question. Likewise, to dismiss the US out of hand is both trendy and trite, a perilous error in the modern world. This book aims to give you a new perspective on a subject that intrigues, outrages, astounds and confounds at every turn. For a country that is mighty in all senses of the word, it nevertheless spawns a wealth of minutiae that lends the nation a broader, deeper foundation.

To prove my point, the bizarre and the fundamental lie randomly, side by side. Alas, if you read and absorb all that is within the covers of this book there will remain a Pacific-sized ocean of facts, figures and fascinating or facetious clips of information still unknown to you. But don't shy away from this challenge. While it's impossible to conquer this sheer edifice of enlightenment, it is enormous fun trying.

LONG WALK

Actress Joanne Woodward was the first to be inscribed upon Hollywood's Walk of Fame. Since her name went down on 9 February 1960, thousands of stars have been honoured by having their name added to the relevant Hollywood boulevards. The number increases at a rate of about one or two a month.

TOP GUNS

During 1999, there were 80 gun-related deaths every day in the United States, an astonishing total of 28,874. Of these, 58 per cent were suicides and 38 per cent homicides (the other 4 per cent were presumably listed as 'don't knows' by coroners). If these figures look bad, at least the trends are getting better. Between 1993 and 1999, gun deaths fell by 27 per cent and in 2000 the wonderfully named National Instant Criminal Background Check System ensured that 136,000 of the 7.8 million applications to buy or transfer firearms were binned. Instant criminals must be shaking in their shoes.

JUST VISITING

America has never been more conscious of securing borders against terrorism, but the practical problems are mind-boggling. Statistics from the United States Customs Service show that, certainly up until 9/11, 60 million people a year arrived on 675,000 commercial and private flights. Another 370 million crossed by land and a further 6 million by sea. Around 116 million vehicles passed over the Canadian and Mexican borders, while more than 90,000 commercial ships docked a total of 9 million containers and 365 million tonnes (400 million tons) of cargo at US ports. Then there were the 157,000 yachts and motorboats that dropped anchor in small town harbours. This all adds up to 436 million annual visitors, roughly 170 million more than the entire permanent population of the country. Picking out the bad guys can therefore be challenging, especially when US Customs deploys barely 7,500 officers across 301 ports of entry.

TRIPLE CHANCES

With odds of 50 million to 1 stacked against her, 19-year-old Crystal Cornick gave birth to her second set of triplets at the University of Maryland Hospital in February 2000.

SMURFIN' USA

Pay more than $10,000 (£6,000) into an American bank and you have to fill out a CTR (Currency Transaction Reporting) form. With the American narcotics market estimated at $57 billion (£34 billion) annually, and banks open 255 days a year, it means that traffickers theoretically need 7,450 couriers each, depositing $223.5 million (£135 million) per day to launder their profits on American soil.

Yet this isn't as fanciful as it might appear. In 1979, when Florida all but disappeared under a cocaine blizzard, the Miami Federal Reserve Bank reported a cash surplus of $5.5 billion (£3.3 billion), more than the other 12 Federal Reserves put together. CTR stopped these drug money deposits for a time, but then Drug Enforcement Agency (DEA) officers noticed how busloads of shady-looking characters with bags stuffed full of more than $9,000 (£5,500) would queue daily outside Florida's banks. The DEA nicknamed them after those cartoon lovables the Smurfs, and to this day 'smurfing' remains in the Agency's lexicon as slang for money laundering.

PRINCESS ON TOUR

Americans love British royalty, but it seems that in 1973 the British were less than enthused about unleashing Princess Margaret (now sadly deceased) onto the US public. According to documents in the UK National Archives, the Brits' ambassador in Washington, Lord Cromer, objected because of the antics of Margaret's entourage during a 1965 visit. In a letter to the Foreign Office committee on royal tours, Lees Mayall, Vice-Marshal of the Diplomatic Service, wrote: 'You will remember that Lord Cromer is not at all keen on having the Princess in the United States, possibly for some time to come. This is mainly due to the behavior of some of HRH's friends, who tend to take such visits very lightly.'

During the 1965 tour, the Princess and her husband (Lord Snowdon) travelled both the east and west coasts of America, popping into Hollywood to meet stars such as Elizabeth Taylor, Paul Newman, Grace Kelly and Judy Garland. Not all of them were impressed. When Margaret told Kelly, aka Princess Grace of Monaco, that she didn't look like a movie star, the irritated actress reportedly replied, 'Well, I wasn't born a movie star.' Judy Garland went even further at a Beverly Hills party when an aide told her that Margaret wanted to hear her sing. Garland made an acid comment about the 'nasty, rude little princess,' but then had second thoughts. 'Tell her I'll sing,' she said, 'if she christens a ship first.'

LOOKING FOR AMERICA

When Art Garfunkel sang of walking off 'to look for America', he wasn't joking. The frizzy-haired icon has a habit of strolling across continents as a way of gathering his thoughts. He has walked coast to coast across the US and, incidentally, also from London to Istanbul.

CALIFORNIA SCHEMIN'

Who says American politicians are dull? Hollywood tough guy Arnold Schwarzenegger's 2003 campaign to become Republican governor of California proved anything but, after reporters dug out cuttings of his old interviews. Throughout the summer, Arnie carefully wooed conservative voters (especially the religious Right) by voicing his opposition to late-term abortion and same-sex marriage. Imagine the surprise, then, when they discovered details of the 57-year-old's own sexual past as revealed by him in a 1977 interview with *Oui*, a magazine published by Playboy.

Oui asked if, like some sportsmen, he abstained from sex the night before a bodybuilding event. Arnie replied: 'I can't sleep before a competition and I'm up all night anyway, so instead of staring at the ceiling I figure I might as well find somebody and f***.' He then referred to a young woman at his gym whom 'everybody jumped on', taking her 'upstairs where we all got together.' Arnie responded to these revelations by insisting he hadn't lived his life to be governor of California. Then he said he made up the orgy story as a publicity stunt. Looks like that worked, then. None of the above scuppered his campaign, and he was duly elected in October 2003.

Not to be outdone, the Democrats also found themselves with a prospective 2004 election candidate in need of careful handling. Step forward trash TV icon Jerry Springer, whose hopes of standing in Ohio for the US Senate were greeted with unrestrained derision by commentators. The *Hotline*, a respected Washington political newsletter, introduced a section titled 'Your Daily Springer', which gleefully reported the happenings on one of Jerry's recent shows: 'Number of times nudity needed to be censored for this episode: nine. Number of fights broken up: ten. Number of lap dances audience members gave guests: two.' Jerry was unrepentant. 'I'm not going to run away from the show,' he said. 'If I articulate a point of view that really relates to just regular, ordinary Americans then I'll be successful.'

WHITE HOUSE BLUES

In 1969, the White House Office of National Drug Control Policy (ONDCP) had a budget of $650 million (£390 million). In 1981 Ronald Reagan increased this to a round $1 billion (£625 million), and by 1999 Bill Clinton had agreed expenditure of $17.1 billion (£10.3 billion). So where's the 'control'? During Clinton's era, someone, somewhere in America was being arrested every 30 seconds on a narcotics charge. One fifth of all inmates in State prisons and two-thirds of all federal prisoners had been found guilty of drug-linked crimes. By 2001, the total annual cost of keeping these criminals locked up was around $8.6 billion (£5.2 billion) and, counting the ONDCP budget, America spent at least $25.7 billion (£15.5 billion) on drug 'control'. Someone needs to tell the traffickers…

JAILHOUSE CRUSH

One of America's most feared prisons, San Quentin, Marin County, California, was opened in 1852 in response to a crime wave sweeping the state. It was built by inmates, who lived in appallingly cramped conditions aboard a prison ship moored at nearby Port Quentin. Things have changed of course, but not that much. According to the California Department of Corrections, San Quentin housed 5,967 prisoners in 2000, including 560 on death row. The design capacity is 3,317.

CHEERS TO THE GIRLS

'Ski-u-mah', 'Hoo-rah' and 'Ra ra ra' were the chants used by America's first ever cheerleader, Johnny Campbell, during a football game at Minnesota University on 2 November 1898. In those days cheerleading was a man's (or a boy's) game, done for the fun of it, but now it's the preserve of muscle-toned teenage girls who regard selection 'try-outs' as a serious business. Their mothers are even pushier. In 1991, a Texan mom called Wanda Holloway hired a contract killer to take out the mother of her daughter's main rival, on the assumption that the resulting grief would scupper the girl's chances. Fortunately, Wanda was rumbled and got a 15-year jail sentence.

VINTAGE YEARS

A poll of 2,000 American film buffs in 2003 suggested that World War II produced some of Hollywood's finest hours. Asked to name the years that produced the best crop of films, 1939, 1940, 1941 and 1942 all figured in the Top 10. The winning years – in order of popularity – were as follows:

1939

Gone With The Wind
Goodbye Mr Chips
Gunga Din
Mr Smith Goes To Washington
Stagecoach
The Wizard Of Oz
Wuthering Heights

1974

Chinatown
The Godfather II
The Great Gatsby
The Man With The Golden Gun
The Odessa File

1946

The Best Years Of Our Lives
The Big Sleep
It's A Wonderful Life
The Killers
My Darling Clementine
Notorious
The Postman Always Rings
   Twice

1941

Citizen Kane
How Green Was My Valley
The Lady Eve
The Maltese Falcon
Sullivan's Travels

1957

The Bridge On The River Kwai
The Enemy Below
Sayonara

1971

A Clockwork Orange
The French Connection
The Last Picture Show
McCabe And Mrs Miller

1940

Fantasia
The Grapes Of Wrath
The Great Dictator
Rebecca

1962

Lawrence Of Arabia
The Manchurian Candidate
To Kill A Mockingbird

1942

Casablanca
Cat People
The Magnificent Ambersons
Now, Voyager
To Be Or Not To Be
Yankee Doodle Dandy

1955

Kiss Me Deadly
The Night Of The Hunter
Rebel Without A Cause

FORD ON THE RIVER

Henry Ford may have been an opinionated, ill-informed anti-Semite (he once declared that all history was bunk), but the mark he left on America's manufacturing industry is undeniable. Born in 1863 on a farm in the suburb of Dearborn (Detroit, Michigan), he founded the Ford Motor Company at the age of 40. His use of the factory assembly line – at one point the Rouge River plant stretched for 11km (7 miles) and employed 81,000 people – made Ford a market leader, and between 1914 and 1916 profits doubled to $60 million (£40 million).

By the time the last of the much-loved Model Ts rolled off the production line in 1927, the company had sold 15 million cars. But Ford was slow to produce new and better designs, and by the 1930s other manufacturers had caught up. Ford himself was said to have regretted the march of industry and longed for the simple, uncomplicated rural idyll of his boyhood, when one in five Michigan citizens lived in Detroit. By the time of his death (1947), this figure had reached three in five.

MASTERS OF THE FIGHT-BACK

In recent years the US Masters at Augusta National has hosted some of the most dramatic final rounds in golfing history. Arguably the five most outstanding performers were:

Gary Player – 1978
By the last day Hubert Green was looking hot favourite to win the coveted Green Jacket, and 42-year-old Player trailed him by seven strokes. But the South African mounted an incredible charge, shooting a winning 64 over the final 18 holes.

Jack Nicklaus – 1986
Sports writers noted that the Golden Bear hadn't won a Major in six years and dismissed him as 'washed-up'. That did the trick for Nicklaus, who overtook a final-round four-stroke lead, carding 30 on the back nine.

Ben Crenshaw – 1995
Crenshaw had won the Masters 11 years earlier, but it remained his only Major championship. In 1995, he was considered a no-hoper still deeply affected by the death of his friend and golf guru Harvey Penick, at whose funeral he'd just served as pallbearer. Despite all this, Crenshaw won the title, dissolving in tears as his last putt sank.

Nick Faldo – 1996
Another of the great comebacks, this time at the expense of Australia's Greg Norman. Six strokes behind on the last day, the British player doggedly refused to accept that he was beaten, completing a superb round of 67 – a stark contrast to Norman's 78.

Tiger Woods – 1997
At 21, Woods became both the youngest and the first non-white winner of the Masters. In the process, he dismantled the tournament record with a four-round total of 271, destroying his opponents with a performance of sheer brilliance. No one got within 12 shots of him.

IF YOU CAN'T BEAT 'EM, EMPLOY 'EM

According to a 1999 report by the Los Angeles Citizens' Commission, the CIA had a 'memorandum of understanding' with the Justice Department which allowed intelligence chiefs to employ drug traffickers and money launderers as agents and subcontractors. 'US government sponsorship of the Contras', the Commission concluded, 'seriously aggravated the flow of cocaine into the United States.'

SUPER BOWL RESULTS SINCE FIRST GAME

Date	Venue	Winner points	Loser points
1967	Los Angeles	Green Bay 35	Kansas City 10
1968	Miami	Green Bay 33	Oakland 14
1969	Miami	New York 16	Baltimore 7
1970	New Orleans	Kansas City 23	Minnesota 7
1971	Miami	Baltimore 16	Dallas 13
1972	New Orleans	Dallas 24	Miami 3
1973	Los Angeles	Miami 14	Washington 7
1974	Houston	Miami 24	Minnesota 7
1975	New Orleans	Pittsburgh 16	Minnesota 6
1976	Miami	Pittsburgh 21	Dallas 17
1977	Pasadena	Oakland 32	Minnesota 14
1978	New Orleans	Dallas 27	Denver 10
1979	Miami	Pittsburgh 35	Dallas 31
1980	Pasadena	Pittsburgh 31	Los Angeles 19
1981	New Orleans	Oakland 27	Philadelphia 10
1982	Pontiac, MI	San Francisco 26	Cincinnati 21
1983	Pasadena	Washington 27	Miami 17
1984	Tampa	Los Angeles 38	Washington 9
1985	Stanford, CA	San Francisco 38	Miami 16
1986	New Orleans	Chicago 46	New England 10
1987	Pasadena	New York 39	Denver 20
1988	San Diego	Washington 42	Denver 10
1989	Miami	San Francisco 20	Cincinnati 16
1990	New Orleans	San Francisco 55	Denver 10
1991	Tampa	New York 20	Buffalo 19
1992	Minneapolis	Washington 37	Buffalo 24
1993	Pasadena	Dallas 52	Buffalo 17
1994	Atlanta	Dallas 30	Buffalo 13
1995	Miami	San Francisco 49	San Diego 26
1996	Tempe, AZ	Dallas 27	Pittsburgh 17
1997	New Orleans	Green Bay 35	New England 21
1998	San Diego	Denver 31	Green Bay 24
1999	Miami	Denver 34	Atlanta 19
2000	Atlanta	St Louis 32	Tennessee 16
2001	Tampa	Baltimore 34	New York 7
2002	New Orleans	New England 20	St Louis 17
2003	San Diego	Tampa Bay 48	Oakland 21

GOD VS AMERICA

Roy 'Moses' Moore, chief justice of Alabama, won celebrity status in his battle to keep a 1.8 tonne (2 ton) granite sculpture of the Ten Commandments outside his state courthouse. It was wheeled away in September 2003 after a federal judge ruled that religion had no place in or around legal institutions.

GREAT MOMENTS IN BASEBALL HISTORY

30 September 1927, Yankee Stadium, New York
Babe Ruth hits his 60th home run in a single season.

28 June 1939, Shibe Park, Philadelphia
The New York Yankees seal a fourth consecutive World Series title.

17 July 1941, Cleveland Stadium
Yankees centre fielder Joe Di Maggio – aka 'Joltin'Joe' – sees his consecutive 56-game home-run hitting streak finally come to an end.

28 September 1941, Shibe Park, Philadelphia
Ted Williams records a final batting average of .406, the first .400+ season average since 1930. No one has emulated the feat since.

18 September 1954, Cleveland Stadium
The Cleveland Indians beat the Detroit Tigers to win their 111th game of the regular season – eight more than the Yankees.

8 October 1956, Yankee Stadium, New York
Game five of the World Series between the Yankees and the Brooklyn Dodgers sees the Yankees' Don Larsen become the first and only pitcher to throw a no-hitter in the World Series – the perfect game – taking 97 pitches to retire 27 Dodger batters.

1 October 1961, Yankee Stadium, New York
Roger Maris hits a fastball into the right-fielding seating to score his 61st home run in a season, just pipping Babe Ruth's record.

6 September 1995, Oriole Park, Baltimore
Cal Ripken completes his 2,131st consecutive game for the Baltimore Orioles, breaking Lou 'Iron Horse' Gehrig's 56-year-old record.

TAKING THE PLEDGE

The original pledge was 'composed' by Francis Bellamy and was published in the *Youth's Companion* in September 1892. It read:

> I pledge allegiance to my Flag,
> And [to*] the Republic for which it stands:
> One Nation indivisible,
> With Liberty and Justice for all.
>
> ** The 'to' was added in October 1892.*

On Columbus Day, October 1892, the Pledge of Allegiance was repeated by more than 12 million public school children in every state in the union. Since then, the wording of the Pledge has been modified three times.

On 14 June 1923, it was amended to read:

> I pledge allegiance to the Flag of the United States,
> And to the Republic for which it stands:
> One Nation indivisible,
> With Liberty and Justice for all.

In 1924, 'of America' was added.

> I pledge allegiance to the Flag
> Of the United States of America,
> And to the Republic for which it stands:
> One Nation indivisible,
> With Liberty and Justice for all.

On Flag Day, 14 June 1954, the words 'under God' were added. So the Pledge of Allegiance now reads:

> I pledge allegiance to the Flag
> Of the United States of America,
> And to the Republic for which it stands:
> One nation under God, indivisible,
> With liberty and justice for all.

In 1945, the Pledge to the Flag received its official title as the Pledge of Allegiance.

When reciting the Pledge, you should stand with your right hand over your heart, fingers together and horizontal with the arm at as near a right angle as possible, and you should be facing the flag. After the Pledge, the arm should drop to the side.

An Army officer or an enlisted person always removes his or her right glove when taking his oath. The Daughters of the American Revolution follow the custom of having the right hand ungloved.

TITANIC TIMELINE

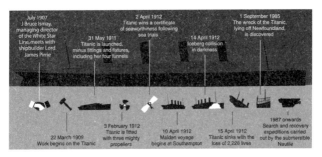

July 1907
J Bruce Ismay, managing director of the White Star Line, meets with shipbuilder Lord James Pirrie

31 May 1911
Titanic is launched, minus fittings and fixtures, including her four funnels

2 April 1912
Titanic wins a certificate of seaworthiness following sea trials

14 April 1912
Iceberg collision in darkness

1 September 1985
The wreck of the Titanic, lying off Newfoundland, is discovered

22 March 1909
Work begins on the Titanic

3 February 1912
Titanic is fitted with three mighty propellers

10 April 1912
Maiden voyage begins at Southampton

15 April 1912
Titanic sinks with the loss of 2,228 lives

1987 onwards
Search and recovery expeditions carried out by the submersible Nautile

NEW MEN

American men are shouldering more domestic chores – according to a University of California national survey of 3,563 families. Researchers found that today's males still do less housework than women, but they have taken on more cooking, cleaning and shopping. They also spend more time with their children than did previous generations – three whole hours on Saturdays and Sundays.

THE HIGH LIFE, 1982-STYLE

In 1982, 10.4 million Americans experimented with cocaine for the first time, more than any previous or subsequent year. According to the US National Drug Control Strategy's 2001 annual report, this figure had dropped to 934,000 first-time users by 1998.

RACIAL MELTDOWN

The 2000 census was the first in which Americans could tick more than five boxes to record their ethnic origin. Instead, there are now 128 racial permutations listed. By 2030, however, there could be bad news for both the bureaucrats and the Ku Klux Klan. Up to 10 per cent of Americans are expected to follow the lead of golfer Tiger Woods and actor Vin Diesel, and refuse to call themselves anything other than multiracial.

SURFING TERMINOLOGY

amped charged up, stoked, fired

backdoor to pull into a tube from behind the peak

bail to abandon a board, jump off, usually with no idea where the board is going next

brah from *bruddah*, Hawaiian Pidgin for 'brother'

bro a buddy or friend

bump a swell

carve symmetrical, fluid turns

clucked afraid, intimidated by the wave

drop in late catch the steepest part of a wave

dropping in catching a wave that is already occupied, taking off on the shoulder while someone is taking off deeper

dune big, peaky wave

full on with commitment and intensity

gash very sharp turn

gnarly awesome and intimidating

going off a break under optimum conditions

grommet adolescent surfer

nipped get nipples rubbed raw by board or suit

pit the hollowest portion of a breaking wave

rip to surf to the height of one's abilities

scabbed getting damaged by a reef or rock

squid unlikeable individual

stoked geared up, wound up, full of enthusiasm

stuffed getting driven under the water by a wave coming down on you

wipeout a fall, particularly a spectacular fall

POKER'S GREATEST GUNSLINGERS

James 'Wild Bill' Hickok

Born	Troy Grove, Illinois, 1837
Reputation	Tough, womanising ex-Union Civil War scout
Downfall	Shot in the back of the head while playing at a Deadwood, South Dakota, saloon in 1876

Legacy   The hand he held that day – two pairs, aces over eights –
              passed into poker folklore as the 'Dead Man's Hand'

Wyatt Earp

Born   Monmouth, Illinois, 1848

Reputation Pro-poker player, bison-hunter, railwayman, fist-fighter,
              mining speculator and on the winning side at the Gunfight
              at the OK Corral

Downfall   More of a gentle decline – he died a natural death in 1929

Legacy   Five Star All-American Wild West Hero

John Henry 'Doc' Holliday

Born   Griffin, Georgia, 1852

Reputation Dentist (hence 'Doc') turned pro-gambler, rarely without knife
              and pistol, possessor of hot temper and veteran of at least
              eight gunfights

Downfall   General ill health (including tuberculosis) – he died in 1883 at
              Glenwood Springs, Colorado, after drinking his morning whisky

Legacy   A gunfighter with humour: his last words – 'This is funny' –
              referred to his incredulity at dying from natural causes rather
              than a bullet

William Barclay 'Bat' Masterson

Born   Iroquois County, Illinois, 1853

Reputation Dancing girls' troupe manager, quick-draw expert and US
              Marshal whose mere presence stifled trouble

Downfall   Became sports editor of the *New York Morning Telegraph*;
              died at his desk in 1921

Legacy   Great frontiersman who, with Wyatt Earp, brought law and
              order to Tombstone, Arizona

Alice Duffield ('Poker' Alice)

Born   Sudbury, Suffolk, England, 1851

Reputation Emigré schoolteacher's daughter and masterful poker player,
              who once shot a man in Deadwood, South Dakota, after he
              accused her husband of cheating

Downfall   A lifetime smoking big cigars – she died of cancer in 1878 at
              Fort Meade, South Dakota

Legacy   Few in the Wild West matched her courage or chutzpah

POWERBALL PARTY

In 1998, America's biggest lottery, the Powerball, offered a $250 million (£151 million) rollover jackpot. The result was traffic mayhem as punters headed for states where tickets were legally available. In Connecticut alone, the bill in overtime for workers in the emergency services topped $85,000 (£51,000).

STARS AND STRIPES

The American flag has 13 horizontal stripes (7 red ones alternating with 6 white) and, in the upper corner bordering the flag's mast, a rectangular blue field with 50 five-pointed white stars in it. The stripes represent the 13 colonies that originally constituted the United States of America, and the stars are the 50 states of the Union. The colours mimicked those of Great Britain, although colonists ultimately sought to distance themselves from the mother country. In the words of the Continental Congress, which defined the symbolic meanings of the colours red, white, and blue (as used in the flag), 'White signifies Purity and Innocence; Red, Hardiness and Valor; and Blue, Vigilance, Perseverance and Justice.' The American flag is frequently called the Star-Spangled Banner, the Stars and Stripes or the Red, White, and Blue. Another popular, patriotic nickname for it is Old Glory, although no one knows why.

STEAMSHIP DISASTERS

8 September 1851 – Waukegan, Illinois
The 910-tonne (1,000-ton) paddle steamer *Lady Elgin* collided with the schooner Augusta. More than 280 people died.

23 January 1856 – North Atlantic
The steamer *Pacific* disappeared. Between 190 and 280 lives were lost.

12 September 1857 – Cape Hatteras, North Carolina
The *Central America*, 90m (300ft) long, with three masts and two steam engines, left Havana, Cuba, for New York with nearly 600 passengers, including many successful gold miners from California. A gale developed which reached hurricane force and the *Central America* developed a leak that eventually extinguished her boiler fires. The following day she foundered and sank. Captain William Herndon went to the wheelhouse and went down with his ship. Only 160 passengers survived. The wreck of the *Central America* was rediscovered in 1988 and the gold recovered in 1989. Valuers calculated that the value of the items recovered was $21 million (£12.6 million) – $9 million (£5.4 million) less than was spent recovering it!

13 June 1858 – Mississippi River, Memphis
Steamboat *Pennsylvania* exploded, causing 150 deaths.

18 October 1865 – Georgia
The *Republic* (formerly the *Tennessee*) sank during a hurricane off the coast of Georgia. Most of the passengers and crew survived, but the $400,000 (£240,000) worth of coins sank with the ship. The wreck has recently been located and, if recovered, it is estimated that the coins will now be worth up to $157 million (£95 million) on the open market.

27 April 1865 – Mississippi River, Memphis
Estimates of the number of people on board the steamboat *Sultana* when it exploded in the Mississippi River, near Memphis, range from about 1,800 to about 2,100 (she was only registered to carry 376, including crew). The *Sultana* was overloaded with northward-bound Union soldiers who had just been released from Confederate prisoner-of-war camps at the end of the Civil War. Three boilers exploded and the flames were so intense that their glow was visible 11km (7 miles) downstream at Memphis. Some of the passengers and crew were able to swim or to lash wood together to form makeshift rafts. A few made it to the *Sultana*'s surviving lifeboats.

3 October 1866 – New York
Steamship *Evening Star* foundered on a journey from New York to New Orleans. About 250 lives were lost.

27 October 1869 – Mississippi River, Illinois
Steamboat *Stonewall* caught fire. Around 200 people died.

25 January 1870 – New York
Steamship *City of Boston* left New York with 117 passengers and was never heard from again.

30 July 1871 – Staten Island
Ferry boat *Westfield* exploded in New York. About 1,000 lives were lost.

4 November 1875 – Cape Flattery
Steamship *Pacific* was in a collision 48km (30 miles) southwest of Cape Flattery, killing 236 people.

31 January 1878 – North Carolina
Steamship *Metropolis* wrecked off North Carolina with 104 lives lost.

18 January 1884 – Gay Head Light, Massachusetts
Steamship *City of Columbus* wrecked off Gay Head Light, Massachusetts, leaving nearly 100 people dead.

STEAMSHIP DISASTERS (CONT'D)

19 April 1884 – Mid Atlantic
The Bark *Ponema* and steamship *State of Florida* sank in mid-ocean after
colliding, with the loss of 145 lives.

30 June 1900 – Hudson River, Hoboken
At about 4:00pm, a fire started among the cotton bales stored at pier 3 in
Hoboken, New Jersey. It could have begun by spontaneous combustion or
a spark from a cigarette. Within a few minutes, a strong wind had spread it
to four ocean liners belonging to the north German Lloyd Steamship
Company. Three burned: the *Saale*, *Bremen* and *Main*. The fourth, the
Kaiser Wilhelm der Grosse, managed to escape the fire. It's difficult to be
sure of the exact number of those who lost their lives – many drowned in
the Hudson River, the intense heat conducted by the steel hulls of the
ships incinerated others, and the portholes of the passenger liners were
too small to allow escape. The official death toll is about 326 people.

22 February 1902 – Golden Gate, off San Francisco
The steamer *City of Rio de Janeiro* struck rocks in dense fog while
returning from the Far East and sank within an hour, killing 104 people.

15 June 1904 – East River, New York City
St Mark's Lutheran Church on East 6th Street held an annual outing to
celebrate the end of the Sunday school year, with more than 1,300 people
boarding the *General Slocum* for a day at Locust Grove on Long Island
Sound. More than 1,000 people died when the *General Slocum* steamship
burst into flames while moving up the East River. When fire broke out it
was discovered that the 3,000 lifejackets on board were rotten and filled
with disintegrated cork, and also that the lifeboats were wired in place and
could not be released. Other boats pulled a few survivors from the water,
but mostly there were bodies – mainly of women and children. The final
death toll stood at 1,021. Captain Van Schaick was put on trial and
convicted of criminal negligence and manslaughter, and was sentenced to
ten years' hard labour in the Sing Sing prison. He served three years
before receiving a pardon from President William H Taft.

12 February 1907 – Long Island Sound
Steamship *Larchmont* was in collision with the *Harry Hamilton* in Long
Island Sound, causing the loss of 183 lives.

24 July 1915 – Chicago River
The steamship *Eastland* was one of several ships chartered by the
Western Electric Company for its annual picnic, due to be attended by
around 7,000 people. As the passengers boarded, it began listing, and

finally capsized with her mooring lines still tied. The final death toll was 844, of which 472 were women, 290 children and 82 men. The *Eastland* was righted and refloated within three weeks. In 1917, she was acquired by the US Government and converted to the gunboat *Willmette*. She was then used as a training ship by the Naval Reserve until after World War II. She was decommissioned on 28 November 1945, and cut up for scrap early in 1947.

FLAG PROTOCOL

In 1942, Congress decided upon a code of conduct for the American flag. Its contents are as follows:

The flag is to be flown from sunrise to sunset in the open.

It should be raised briskly and lowered with ceremony.

Weather permitting, it is expected to be waving on the mast of or near the main administration buildings of all public institutions, particularly on public holidays.

The flag, when carried in a procession or with another flag or flags, should be on the marching right.

If there is a line of other flags, it should be at the centre of the line formed by the other standards.

No other flag should be placed above the US flag.

When displayed flat on a speaker's platform, the flag should be behind and above the head of the speaker.

There are further rules to regulate the display of the flag at various public ceremonies and in connection with state and city flags and in churches. Other rules deal with the observance of proper respect for the American flag. The latter are supplemented in most of the states by laws prohibiting the use of the US flag for advertising purposes.

The Army, Navy and Air Force have detailed regulations for military and naval uses of the flag.

SHARK ATTACK!

According to George Burgess, Director of the University of Florida's International Shark Attack File, 'Falling coconuts kill 150 people worldwide each year, 15 times the number of fatalities attributable to sharks.'

ISAF statistics for the USA locations with the highest shark attack activity since 1990:

UNITED STATES (437)

YEAR	Total	Fatal	Non-fatal
1990	19	0	19
1991	25	1	24
1992	24	1	23
1993	21	0	21
1994	32	1	31
1995	45	0	45
1996	20	0	20
1997	31	0	31
1998	29	1	28
1999	37	0	37
2000	54	1	53
2001	53	3	50
2002	47	0	47

FLORIDA (289)

YEAR	Total	Fatal	Non-fatal
1990	10	0	10
1991	13	0	13
1992	12	0	12
1993	10	0	10
1994	24	0	24
1995	31	0	31
1996	13	0	13
1997	25	0	25
1998	22	1	21
1999	25	0	25
2000	38	1	37
2001	37	1	36
2002	29	0	29

HAWAII (44)

YEAR	Total	Fatal	Non-fatal
1990	2	0	2
1991	4	1	3
1992	8	2	6
1993	5	0	5
1994	4	0	4
1995	1	0	1
1996	2	0	2
1997	1	0	1
1998	1	0	1
1999	5	0	5
2000	2	0	2
2001	3	0	3
2002	6	0	6

CALIFORNIA (34)

YEAR	Total	Fatal	Non-fatal
1990	4	0	4
1991	4	0	4
1992	1	0	1
1993	4	0	4
1994	2	1	1
1995	3	0	3
1996	3	0	3
1997	1	0	1
1998	2	0	2
1999	2	0	2
2000	3	0	3
2001	1	0	1
2002	4	0	4

In July 1916, over a period of less than two weeks, one or more sharks killed four swimmers and badly injured another off the coast of New Jersey. What made these attacks unusual was the fact that they not only occurred in close proximity to the shore, but also in Matawan Creek, a small stream over 18km (11 miles) inland from the open ocean. This set off a wave of panic that kept visitors out of the water and seriously threatened New Jersey's tourist economy. These attacks became the basis of Peter Benchley's novel *Jaws*. The first fatality (1 July) was Charles Epting Vansant, aged 23. The second was Charles Bruder, attacked as he swam 120m (400ft) off the beach five days later. His legs were torn off just below the knee and his left side was gashed. Beach towns up and down the coastline hurriedly erected steel 'shark nets' to protect bathers, and President Wilson committed the Coast Guard to join in hunting down marauding sharks off the coast. The next attacks were at Matawan Creek, where Lester Stillwell, aged 10, and Stanley Fisher, a 25-year-old local who tried to save him, were killed. A few days later, a 2.5m (8ft) white shark was caught off Sandy Hook with 7kg (15lb) of human flesh in its gut.

In July 2001, Jessie Arbogast, aged 8, was playing in knee-deep water just off Pensicola when he was attacked by a bull shark, that bit off his arm. His uncle carried the boy ashore and returned to the water to wrestle the shark to the shore, where it was shot in the head four times by a park ranger. Using forceps, a volunteer firefighter retrieved the boy's arm from the shark. It was then put on ice, until surgeons reattached it during an 11-hour operation.

THE PRESIDENT'S PANTS

US Navy-issue underpants worn by John F Kennedy during World War II fetched $5,000 (£3,000) at a New Jersey auction in 2003. The 84cm- (33 inch-) waist boxer shorts were catalogued as follows: 'White cotton with snap closures and drawstring waist. Sewn label Jack Kennedy in red with laundry number S 3980 stamped twice on inner waistband.' Auctioneer Paula Hantman delicately pointed out that because Jack's jocks had laundry labels, they'd probably been worn. Presumably washed since 1945, though. The buyer was Irish businessman Paul Allen.

STRONG ARM TACTICS

Governor Jesse Ventura, who was elected governor of Minnesota in 1998, was formerly a WWF professional wrestler.

LONELY SPY

Former military communications officer Jeffrey Carney – codenamed The Kid by his East German handlers – betrayed America for 12 years before defecting to East Berlin in 1984. The US Secret Service snatched him back in 1991 after the fall of the Berlin Wall, and Carney served 11 years of a 20-year sentence. Despite Carney's German citizenship, Berlin later refused his application to emigrate, and by July 2003 he was eking out a meagre living at an Ohio plastics factory. 'I don't much like America,' he told newsmen. 'I'm so lonely I've bought a cat.'

IN MEMORY OF JFK

Assassinated president John F Kennedy, shot dead in Dallas in November 1963, has been posthumously honoured in numerous ways. Here are ten places named after him:

JFK airport in New York

NASA Kennedy Space Center

John F Kennedy School of Government (KSG) at Harvard University

Kennedy Institute of Ethics at Georgetown University in Washington, DC

John F Kennedy Center for the Performance Arts in Washington, DC

Kennedy Krieger Institute in Baltimore, devoted to young people with developmental disabilities

John F Kennedy Center for Research on Human Development at the Vanderbilt University in Nashville, Tennessee

Kennedy Memorial Hospitals, a hospital chain

John F Kennedy High School in Fremont, California

NUCLEAR MISSION

The world's first nuclear power station was opened in 1951 in Idaho, producing electricity generated by a new generation breeder reactor.

The world's largest solar-powered power station in the Mohave Desert, California, is drenched in sufficient sunlight to power two 80-megawatt plants.

MANHATTAN SKYLINE

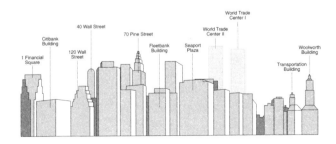

MOTHER LOVE

The B-29 aircraft that carried the atomic bomb 'Little Boy' to Hiroshima was named 'Enola Gay' after the mother of pilot Paul Tibbets.

CLOWNING AROUND

Ronald McDonald appeared in small-screen advertising for the first time in 1967

PRESIDENTIAL 'FIRSTS'

Andrew Jackson: First to ride a train
Abraham Lincoln: First to be photographed in the White House
Rutherford Hayes: First to use a telephone in the White House
Benjamin Harrison: First to use electric lights in the White House
Warren Harding: First to talk on the radio
Franklin Roosevelt: First to appear on television
Dwight Eisenhower: First to fly in a helicopter
Lyndon Johnson: First to make a long-distance call using satellite

CROMWELL'S DOOM

The US city of Huntington, New York, apparently named after Oliver Cromwell's birthplace, banned his family's lion crest from its civic coat of arms in protest at the Lord Protector's treatment of the Irish during the English Civil War. Cynics point out that, as Cromwell was born in Huntingdon (with a 'd'), Cambridgeshire, the whole lion thing was obviously flawed from the start.

THE THINGS THEY SAY ABOUT AMERICA

'America, thou half-brother of the world;
With something good and bad of every land'
Philip James Bailey

'America is a large, friendly dog in a very small room. Every time it wags its tail, it knocks over a chair.'
Arnold Toynbee

'The United States is a nation of laws; badly written and randomly enforced.'
Frank Zappa

'England and America are two countries separated by a common language.'
George Bernard Shaw

'In the United States there is more space where nobody is than where anybody is. That is what makes America what it is.'
Gertrude Stein, *The Geographical History Of America*

'In a country as big as the United States, you can find fifty examples of anything.'
Jeffery F Chamberlain

'America is a vast conspiracy to make you happy.'
John Updike, *Problems And Other Stories*

'Terrorist attacks can shake the foundations of our biggest buildings, but they cannot touch the foundation of America. These acts shatter steel, but they cannot dent the steel of American resolve.'
George W Bush, address to the US after hijack attacks on the US World Trade Center and Pentagon, 11 September 2001

'You, the Spirit of the Settlement!... Not understand that America is God's crucible, the great melting pot where all the races of Europe are melting and re-forming! Here, you stand, good folk, think I, when I see them at Ellis Island, here you stand in your fifty groups, with your fifty languages and histories, and your fifty blood hatreds and rivalries.'
Israel Zangwill, *The Melting Pot*

'The entire essence of America is the hope to first make money – then make money with money – then make lots of money with lots of money.'
Paul Erdman (novelist)

'Then join hand in hand, brave Americans all! By uniting we stand, by
dividing we fall.'
John Dickinson, *The Liberty Song*

'Kill my boss? Do I dare live out the American dream?'
Homer Simpson

FAMOUS LA BUILDINGS

810 Linden Drive, Beverly Hills
Bugsy Siegel, famous mobster, was shot and killed here shortly before
midnight on 20 June 1947. Siegel is widely acclaimed as the man who built
Las Vegas. His hotel, the Flamingo, was the first super-hotel to be built on
the now-famous Las Vegas strip, then just a dirt-track.

730 North Bedford Drive, Beverly Hills
It was here, on 5 April 1958, that Lana Turner's daughter Cheryl Crane
stabbed and killed Lana's boyfriend, Johnny Stompanato. Although ruled
a justifiable homicide, people have always queried how a 14-year-old girl
could overpower a 80kg (175lb) man, and what role Lana herself played
in the killing...

12305 Fifth Helena, Brentwood
The house where Marilyn Monroe died.

625 Beach Road, PCH, Santa Monica
Peter Lawford's beach home was the place where Marilyn Monroe and
President John F Kennedy carried on their secret affair in the early 1960s.

516 Walden Drive, Beverly Hills
Built in 1921 for a movie studio in Culver City, it was used in several films
until 1926, when it was moved to Beverly Hills. It has been a private home
ever since. It looks just like a fairy-tale cottage and it has become known as
the 'Witch's House'.

565 North Cahuenga, Hancock Park
Used as the Cunninghams' home in the TV series *Happy Days*.

14611 Sutton Street, Sherman Oaks
James Dean's last home.

1270 Tower Grove Road, Beverly Hills
The house from which Heidi Fleiss ran a brothel that was frequented by
many of the rich and famous.

HIGHS AND LOWS

An independent poll contrived a league table of presidents. Each was judged on leadership qualities, accomplishments and crisis management, political acumen, appointments and general character. Here is the poll's Top 10:

1. Abraham Lincoln
2. Franklin Roosevelt
3. George Washington
4. Thomas Jefferson
5. Theodore Roosevelt
6. Woodrow Wilson
7. Harry Truman
8. Andrew Jackson
9. Dwight Eisenhower
10. James Madison

And the Bottom 10:

30. Richard Nixon
31. Calvin Coolidge
32. John Tyler
33. William Harrison
34. Millard Fillmore
35. Franklin Pierce
36. Ulysses Grant
37. Andrew Johnson
38. James Buchanan
39. Warren Harding

Note: Bill Clinton and both Bush Presidents were excluded from the poll.

10 TALLEST BUILDINGS IN THE US

Building (city)	Height	Number of storeys	Built
Sears Tower (Chicago)	442m (1,450ft)	110	1974
Tallest building in the world until 1997			
World Trade Center I/II (New York City)	417/415m (1,368/1,362ft)	110	1972/ 1973
Tallest tower in the world until the completion of the Sears Tower; destroyed by terrorists 2001			
Empire State Building (New York City)	381m (1,250ft)	102	1931
Tallest building in the world 1931–77			

Amoco (Chicago)	346m (1,136ft)	80	1973
John Hancock Center (Chicago)	343m (1,127ft)	100	1969
Chrysler Building (New York City)	319m (1,046ft)	77	1930
NationsBank Tower (Atlanta)	312m (1,023ft)	55	1992
Library Tower (Los Angeles)	310m (1,018ft)	73	1990
AT&T Corporation Center (Chicago)	307m (1,007ft)	61	1989
Chase Tower (Houston)	305m (1,002ft)	75	1982

BLACK SEPTEMBER

The greatest blackout in American history occurred in September 2003, when anything up to 50 million consumers across the northeastern states, together with southern Canada, lost electricity for 24 hours. The cause was linked to a fault in high-voltage lines near Cleveland, compounded by the failure of an alarm system. One overloaded line sagged, then hit a tree and set off a chain reaction, resulting in massive power surges across the grid. As a result, power stations automatically shut themselves down. The only real winners were New York City cops, who made 850 arrests over the blackout period – 100 fewer than the norm.

BAD HABITS

American actress Tallulah Bankhead arguably delivered her greatest one-liner off camera. The daughter of Democratic Party leader and House of Representatives speaker William Brockman Bankhead would take cocaine by dropping a solution in her eyes. When later asked about the addiction risks, she reportedly replied, 'Cocaine isn't habit-forming. I should know, I've been using it for years.'

DOOMED JOURNEYS

Will Rogers, 15 August 1935
Born in 1879, Rogers appeared in the Ziegfeld Follies for ten years and in 70 Hollywood movies. He died in a plane crash in Alaska.

Amelia Earhart, 2 July 1937
Taking off from Oakland, California in May 1937, Earhart intended to be the first person to pilot a plane around the world on an equatorial route. On 2 July, she was supposed to land at Howland Island in the South Pacific, but she and her navigator, Fred Noonan, never arrived. The last transmission from Earhart was heard at 8:43am local time. Neither she nor her plane was ever seen again.

Tom Mix (silent film star), 12 October 1940
Tom was speeding across Arizona in his roadster when he unexpectedly encountered a bridge under construction. While braking and swerving to avoid the bridge, Mix dislodged a heavy suitcase from the luggage rack behind him. The suitcase crashed forward into his head, and killed him.

Carole Lombard, 17 January 1942
Child star Lombard was a Hollywood sweetheart and the wife of actor Clark Gable. Her death in an air disaster came as she flew from the Midwest to California following a patriotic tour selling US bonds.

Glenn Miller, 15 December 1944
On a cloudy December day in 1944, Miller took off from England in a small plane, and headed for Paris to make arrangements for a concert. No trace of Miller or his plane was ever found.

Margaret Mitchell (author of *Gone With The Wind*), 11 August 1949
Mitchell was crossing an Atlanta street on her way to the theatre when a speeding cab hit her. She died of her injuries five days later.

James Dean, 30 September 1955
Driving his new car, a Porsche Spyder, on the way to a race in Salinas, California, Dean crashed head-on into a second car. His passenger was thrown clear and survived, but Dean died almost immediately. He was just 24 years old.

Jackson Pollock, 11 August 1956
Pollock was driving his Cadillac between taverns near his home on Long Island, New York, and was killed in a car crash.

Buddy Holly, Ritchie Valens and **The Big Bopper**, 3 February 1959
The plane carrying the three touring stars crashed, leaving no survivors.

Eddie Cochran, 17 April 1960
Cochran was killed in Chippenham, England, when his taxi suffered a burst tyre, veered off the road and crashed. Gene Vincent was a badly injured passenger. Cochran was only 21.

US Olympic figure skating team, 15 February 1961
The team were passengers on a Belgian Sabena Boeing 707 that crashed near Brussels, Belgium. The accident killed 72 passengers, as well as a farmer on the ground.

Patsy Cline, 5 March 1963
Patsy's lover and manager, Randy Hughes, flew Patsy to Kansas City for a benefit for the widow of a country disc jockey who had died in a car crash. The return journey was hampered by storms and poor visibility, and the plane crashed in swamped woodlands in Camden, Tennessee, 135km (85 miles) from Nashville. Another country star, Jack Anglin (of the duo Johnny And Jack), was killed on the way to her funeral.

Jim Reeves, 31 July 1964
He flew with pianist Dean Manuel to Batesville, Arkansas, on 30 July 1964. The next day, while approaching Nashville on his return, the plane ran into a rainstorm and disappeared from radar. It took two days to find the wreckage and the bodies.

Jayne Mansfield, 29 June 1967
She was driving from Biloxi, Mississippi, to New Orleans at about 2:00am, rushing to make a talk-show appearance in New Orleans the next morning. Mansfield was in the front seat with her lawyer Sam Brody and a chauffeur, when their Cadillac ran into the back of a truck that was spraying for mosquitoes. Mansfield, Brody and the chauffeur were killed, but her three children, who were riding in the back seat, survived.

Otis Redding and **The Bar-Kays**, 10 December 1967
The Bar-Kays - Jimmy King (guitar), Ronnie Caldwell (organ), Phalin Jones (saxophone) and Carl Cunningham (drums) - were employed as Otis Redding's backing group on tour. The light aircraft in which they were travelling plunged into Lake Monona, Madison, Wisconsin. Otis had recorded '(Sittin' On) The Dock Of The Bay' just three days earlier, and it became his only million-seller and US pop Number One.

Natalie 'Dolly' Sinatra, 6 January 1977
Frank Sinatra's mother, Dolly, was one of four people who died in the crash of a Gates Lear jet, which flew into a mountain shortly after taking off from Palm Springs Municipal Airport in California.

DOOMED JOURNEYS (CONT'D)

Mary Jo Kopechne, 18 July 1969
Mary Jo was in the passenger seat of the car driven by Senator Edward Kennedy that flipped off the Dike Bridge and into a large pond. She was trapped in the car and died at the scene. Kennedy escaped but he failed to report the accident until the next morning. This led to a public scandal and ruined his plans to run for president in 1972.

Rocky Marciano, 31 August 1969
Born Rocco Marchegiano, he took his first world heavyweight championship title in 1952 and defended it six times before he retired four years later. He was unbeaten in his 49 professional fights, and eventually died in an air crash.

Grace Kelly/Princess Grace of Monaco, 15 September 1982
Grace Kelly was a successful Hollywood actress before abandoning her career to marry Prince Rainier of Monaco in 1956. In 1982, probably due to a minor stroke while driving, she lost control of her car. It veered off the road and rolled down a cliff-side, injuring the princess and her younger daughter Stephanie. Stephanie recovered, but Princess Grace died the next day.

Senator **John Heinz** and former Senator **John Tower**, 4 and 5 April 1991
Both men died in unrelated plane accidents within a day of each other. At least 16 other US senators and members of Congress have died in plane crashes.

John Denver, 12 October 1997
Denver was killed instantly in the crash, shortly after takeoff, of the Long-EZ experimental aeroplane he was piloting to Monterey Bay. Denver, an experienced pilot, had taken delivery of the Y-shaped, futuristic-looking plane just a day before the crash.

John F Kennedy Jr, his wife **Carolyn Bessette Kennedy** and her sister **Lauren Bessette**, 16 July 1999
They were killed when their Piper Saratoga II HP crashed into the ocean off Martha's Vineyard. They had been on their way to a family wedding.

COFFIN COUNT

For almost half a century, the US government claimed 54,246 of its troops were killed during the Korean War. However, when officials took a close look at statistics in June 2000 they discovered that the true figure was, in fact, 36,940.

RANDOM FACTS YOU NEVER KNEW ABOUT NATIVE AMERICANS

- There are 26 states with names of Native American origin: Alabama, Alaska, Arizona, Arkansas, Connecticut, Idaho, Illinois, Iowa, Kansas, Kentucky, Massachusetts, Michigan, Minnesota, Mississippi, Missouri, Nebraska, New Mexico, North Dakota, Ohio, Oklahoma, South Dakota, Tennessee, Texas, Utah, Wisconsin, Wyoming.
- During World War II, the Japanese army could not break the 'secret code' of the US Military. This 'secret code' was simply a group of Navajo volunteers speaking their Native American language on their field radios!
- The Navajo are the largest Native American tribe and have a reservation that stretches across three states, with an area of more than 65,000 square km (25,000 square miles).
- Oklahoma is the state with the largest Native American population.
- Jim Thorpe is probably the most famous Native American athlete. On winning an Olympic medal in Sweden in 1912, the King of Sweden said to him, 'You, sir, are the greatest athlete in the world.'
- The Pontiac car was named after the chief of the Ottawa Indians.
- All American Indians officially became US citizens in 1924.
- In 1639, Jonas Bronck bought the area now known as the Bronx for 'two guns, two kettles, two coats, two shirts, one barrel of cider, and six bits of money'.
- Early Spanish missionaries offered flannel underwear to Native Americans in the hope of spreading European values!

BURGER BIRTHPLACE

The first McDonald's restaurant opened in 1955 in Des Plaines, Illinois, as a result of milkshake maker Ray Kroc joining forces with Californian hamburger stall owners Dick and Mac McDonald. Takings on the first day amounted to $366.12 (£220.55). Kroc inspired staff with his catchphrase, 'If you've got time to lean, you've got time to clean.' The enterprise was such a roaring success that McDonald's became a public company in 1965 and is today among the 30 companies listed in the Dow Jones index.

Meanwhile, the building in Des Plaines where fast food was pioneered is now a museum.

WHO SHOT BUGSY SIEGEL?

Bugsy Siegel is the man who cemented the Mob's relationship with Las Vegas. His dream was to create America's most luxurious gambling hotel, the Flamingo, and he assembled a consortium of godfathers led by his childhood buddies back east, Meyer Lansky and Charlie 'Lucky' Luciano. The original estimate was $1.2 million (£720,000), but construction materials were expensive after the war, and the Teamsters' Union – itself not unconnected with the Mafia – presided over neat scams such as the 'Palm Tree Shuttle', in which trees were hauled to and from California and sold to Siegel several times over. By December 1946 – just 12 months after work started – the project was in crisis. Building costs had risen to $6 million (£3.6 million).

Lansky called his fellow mobsters together and accused Siegel of double-crossing them over the budget. He suggested Bugsy be wiped out, yet (curiously) appears to have worked behind the scenes to give his old friend time to pull the Flamingo around. For a while this worked: in May 1947 the hotel even reported half-year profits of $250,000 (£150,000). But it was too little, too late for Siegel. At 10:30pm on 10 June, as he sat reading the paper at his Hollywood home, a lone gunman raked the nearby window with bullets. One took Siegel in the head, while four more lodged in his lungs. The killer was never caught, although most Mafia historians believe the contract was given to a ruthless professional hitman called Charlie Fischetti. As to the Flamingo, it was sold and eventually relaunched with 'clean' money. It now has 3,500 rooms and ranks among the ten biggest hotels in the world.

APOLLO SPACE MISSIONS

Apollo 1

Apollo 204 was scheduled to be the first manned Apollo mission, but tragedy struck on the launch pad during a pre-flight test. It would have been launched on 21 February 1967, but Astronauts Virgil Grissom, Edward White and Roger Chaffee lost their lives when a fire swept through the command module. In the spring of 1967, NASA's Associate Administrator for Manned Space Flight, Dr George E Mueller, announced that the mission originally scheduled for Grissom, White and Chaffee would be known as Apollo 1.

Mission:	Apollo 7
Lunar module:	Not flown
Command and service module:	Apollo 7
Launch date:	11 October 1968
Mission length:	260 hours, 9 minutes, 3 seconds
Retrieval ship:	*USS Essex*
Crew:	Walter M Schirra, Jr, commander
	Donn F Eisele, command module pilot
	Walter Cunningham, lunar module pilot

Apollo 7 was the first manned test of the command and service module.

Mission:	Apollo 8
Lunar module:	Not flown
Command and service module:	Apollo 8
Launch date:	21 December 1968
Mission length:	146 hours, 59 minutes, 49 seconds
Retrieval ship:	*USS Yorktown*
Crew:	Frank Borman, commander
	James A Lovell, command module pilot
	William A Anders, lunar module pilot

Mission:	Apollo 9
Lunar module:	Spider
Command and service module:	Gumdrop
Launch date:	3 March 1969
Mission length:	241 hours, 0 minutes, 53 seconds
Retrieval ship:	*USS Guadalcanal*
Crew:	James R McDivitt, commander
	David R Scott, command module pilot
	RL Schweikart, lunar module pilot

APOLLO SPACE MISSIONS (CONT'D)

Mission:	Apollo 10
Lunar module:	Snoopy
Command and service module:	Charlie Brown
Launch date:	18 May 1969
Mission length:	192 hours, 3 minutes, 23 seconds
Retrieval ship:	*USS Princeton*
Crew:	Thomas P Stafford, commander
	John W Young, command module pilot
	Eugene A Cernan, lunar module pilot

Mission:	Apollo 11
Lunar module:	Eagle
Command and service module:	Columbia
Launch date:	16 July 1969
Landed on Moon:	20 July 1969
Mission length:	195 hours, 18 minutes, 35 seconds
Retrieval ship:	*USS Hornet*
Crew:	Neil Armstrong, commander
	Michael Collins, command module pilot
	Edwin ('Buzz') Aldrin, lunar module pilot

The prime mission objective of Apollo 11 was simply to 'perform a manned lunar landing and return'. A plaque was fixed to the leg of the lunar landing vehicle signed by President Nixon, Neil Armstrong, Michael Collins and Edwin Aldrin, Jr. The plaque shows a map of the Earth and this inscription:

HERE MEN FROM THE PLANET EARTH
FIRST SET FOOT UPON THE MOON
JULY 1969 AD
WE CAME IN PEACE FOR ALL MANKIND

Mission:	Apollo 12
Lunar module:	Intrepid
Command and service module:	Yankee Clipper
Launch date:	14 November 1969
Landed on Moon:	Nov 19th 1969
Mission length:	244 hours, 36 minutes, 24 seconds
Retrieval ship:	*USS Hornet*
Crew:	Charles Conrad Jr, commander
	Richard Gordon, command module pilot
	Alan Bean, lunar module pilot

Mission:	Apollo 13
Lunar module:	Aquarius
Command and service module:	Odyssey
Launch date:	11 April 1970
Landed on Moon:	Mission aborted
Mission length:	142 hours, 54 minutes, 41 seconds
Retrieval ship:	*USS Iwo Jima*
Crew:	James Lovell Jr, commander
	John Swigert, command module pilot
	Fred Haise, lunar module pilot

Apollo 13 was the first aborted Apollo mission

Mission:	Apollo 14
Lunar module:	Antares
Command and service module:	Kitty Hawk
Launch date:	31 January 1971
Landed on Moon:	5 February 1971
Mission length:	216 hours, 1 minute, 58 seconds
Retrieval ship:	*USS New Orleans*
Crew:	Alan Shepard Jr, commander
	Stuart Roosa, command module pilot
	Edgar Mitchell, lunar module pilot

Mission:	Apollo 15
Lunar module:	Falcon
Command and service module:	Endeavour
Launch date:	26 July 1971
Landed on Moon:	30 July 1971
Mission length:	295 hours, 11 minutes, 53 seconds
Retrieval ship:	*USS Okinawa*
Crew:	David Scott, commander
	Alfred Worden, command module pilot
	James Irwin, lunar module pilot

APOLLO SPACE MISSIONS (CONT'D)

Mission:	Apollo 16
Lunar module:	Orion
Command and service module:	Casper
Launch date:	16 April 1972
Landed on Moon:	21 April 1972
Mission length:	265 hours, 51 minutes, 5 seconds
Retrieval ship:	*USS Ticonderoga*
Crew:	John Young, commander
	Thomas Mattingley II, command module pilot
	Charles Duke Jr, lunar module pilot

Mission:	Apollo 17
Lunar module:	Challenger
Command and service module:	America
Launch date:	7 December 1972
Landed on Moon:	11 December 1972
Mission length:	301 hours, 51 minutes, 59 seconds
Retrieval ship:	*USS Ticonderoga*
Crew:	Eugene Cernan, commander
	Ronald Evans, command module pilot
	Harrison Schmitt, lunar module pilot

Eugene Cernan, commander of Apollo 17, holds the distinction of being the last man to walk on the Moon.

NEVER TOO OLD

The great US jazz altosax player Benny Carter never quite got to grips with the notion of retirement. Born in the Bronx in 1907, he reserved his best work until late in life, signing a new recording contract on his 80th birthday, collecting a Grammy award at 85, another at 87, and cutting an album with Oscar Peterson at 90. When he died (aged 95), friends attributed his longevity to the fact that he was always busy, never worried, never lost his temper and always travelled first class.

THE KNOWLEDGE

During 2002, 24.2 million visitors poured through the doors of the 16 museums run by The Smithsonian Institution. A further 18 million people visited the 129 museums affiliated to The Smithsonian.

SMITH AND WESSON REVOLVER

Founded in 1852 by Horace Smith and DB Wesson, the company is one of the world's most famous brands of firearms. The Smith and Wesson Model 10 is the only gun in continuous production since it was introduced in 1899.

PIPE DREAM

College student Luke Helder planted pipe bombs across the United States in an apparently motiveless series of attacks. Only when police arrested Helder in May 2002 did they discover that he was aiming to draw a big, explosive smiley face across America. Helder, from Minnesota, had planted pipe bombs in Nebraska, Illinois, Iowa, Texas and Colorado before he was captured. Prompt police action meant he was unable to finish the sour smile.

TRAUMA DRAMA

When Californian Steven Dworman was divorced, he decided to turn the domestic trauma into an all-singing, all-dancing production. At a cost of some $1.5 million (£900,000 million), he produced *Divorce: The Musical*, which attracted an audience of thousands when it was screened in a Santa Monica cinema during 2002.

UNCLE SAM AND THE COLOMBIAN MARCHING POWDER

It's a wonder Uncle Sam doesn't need a nose job. According to the UN's Global Illicit Drug Trends report (2001), American law enforcement forces seized 132,318kg (291,000lb) of cocaine in 1999. Their colleagues in Colombia – probably the world's biggest producer – managed to confiscate less than half this amount: 63,945kg (140,000lb). The Mexican police and military came third, with a mere 34,623kg (76,000lb).

Around half of all America's cocaine seizures are made along the 3,200km (2,000 mile) US–Mexico border, a desolate and mostly unfenced desert across which a Panzer division could roll without being spotted. That said, drug smugglers usually prefer the handful of congested, cross-border tarmac roads, where it's easy to blend in to the commercial and holiday traffic. San Ysidro, south of San Diego, is the world's busiest land border crossing, handling 20,000 pedestrians and 96,000 car passengers every day.

Unsurprisingly, US Customs are now heavily dependent on the nation's boffins for some whizzo technical support. They deploy equipment such as density-busters – a kind of ultrasound scanner which decides whether your tyres contain things more interesting than air – and digital cameras which compare 40,000 number plates per day against a national database of suspect vehicles. A few coke runners do try gatecrashing, but the metal tyre shredders that emerge James Bond-style from the road do work pretty well.

In fact, the most sophisticated drug detector known to man is the sniffer dog. Smugglers have tried to fool these creatures by packing consignments into everything from onions to detergent powder, and US Customs tell how one canny trafficker even vacuum-sealed his cocaine, covered the package in grease, sealed it again and then sunk the result inside a car petrol tank. It made no difference: a dog found the stash inside six minutes.

Yet, as detection gets more sophisticated, so the drug runners get more creative. On 26 February 2001, customs officers discovered a 7.6m- (25ft-) long hand-dug tunnel beneath a bungalow in Nogales, Arizona, just 1km (3/4 mile) from the Mexican border. The tunnel was linked to the city's sewer system. Around 200 bricks of cocaine were stored on the property.

AROUND AMERICA IN 13 FILM TITLES

Atlantic City (1980), starring Burt Lancaster and Susan Sarandon. Ageing crook teams up with happy hippie to outwit the Mob.

The Boston Strangler (1968), starring Tony Curtis and Henry Fonda. Story of a savage killer.

Chicago (2002), starring Renée Zellweger, Catherine Zeta Jones and Richard Gere. Musical about notorious women and their quest for fame.

Dodge City (1939), starring Errol Flynn and Olivia de Havilland. Epic Western.

The Cincinnati Kid (1965), starring Steve McQueen and Edward G Robinson. Poker players meet for crunch game in New Orleans.

LA Confidential (1997), starring Russell Crowe, Guy Pearce and Kevin Spacey. Disparate cops unite to halt a string of ruthless killings.

Meet Me In St Louis (1944), starring Judy Garland and Margaret O'Brien. Musical family drama.

Mr Smith Goes To Washington (1939), starring James Stewart and Jean Arthur. Honest senator from Hicksville challenges political sleaze.

New York, New York (1977), starring Liza Minnelli and Robert De Niro. Love affair between musicians turns sour.

Pearl Harbor (2001), starring Ben Affleck and Kate Beckinsale. Complicated romance blossoms among the carnage.

Philadelphia (1993), starring Tom Hanks and Denzel Washington. A gay lawyer battles the effects of AIDS to keep his job.

Sleepless In Seattle (1993) starring Tom Hanks and Meg Ryan. A widower finds new love across the time zones.

Viva Las Vegas (1963), starring Elvis Presley and Ann-Margret. Would-be racing driver forced to sing for his supper.

SOW UNLUCKY

An alarmed walker in Arie Crown Woods, Iowa, alerted the fire brigade when he discovered a drum that apparently contained chemicals. Cautious firefighters were both relieved and appalled to find that the drum was in fact full of pig semen, ostensibly the property of a company called Swine Genetics. The company could offer no explanation of how it had gone astray.

BEATING THE CASINO

Gambling's greatest hero of the 20th century was Edward Thorp, a maths professor at the University of California, whose 1962 book *Beat The Dealer* provided a mathematically proven system of getting a two per cent odds advantage over the House at blackjack. He showed that, because played hands are not returned for shuffling, a trained card counter can work out what's due to be dealt and bet accordingly. Although the dealer should win more hands, the player will win more money by placing big bets at the right time. Casinos responded by keeping six packs in play and ordering croupiers not to deal down to the bottom. They needn't have worried. Few players had the patience or memory to apply Thorp's system properly, and in Nevada – spiritual home of card gamblers – the casinos logged record profits.

PRESIDENTS ON FILM

Lincoln

Abraham Lincoln has been portrayed by, amongst others, Walter Huston, Henry Fonda, Sam Waterston, Raymond Massey, Royal Dano, Gregory Peck, George Billings and Robert V Barron. However, by far the most prolific portrayer of Abraham Lincoln was Frank McGlynn Sr, who spent more years playing Abe than Abe spent being president. Glynn appeared as Abe in all of the following films:

Are We Civilized (1934)
The Littlest Rebel (1935)
Hearts In Bondage (1936)
The Prisoner Of Shark Island (1936)
Western Gold (1937)
Wells Fargo (1937)
The Plainsman (1937)
The Mad Empress (1940)
Hi-Yo Silver (1940) – and, yes, this was a Lone Ranger film!

Kennedy

Cliff Robertson – *PT 109* (1963) as the future President Kennedy
Robert Hogan – *Prince Jack* (1984)
Steve Reed – *JFK* (1991) and *Malcolm X* (1992)
James F Kelly – *Sinatra* (1992)
Bob Gill – *Love Field* (1992)
William Peterson – *The Rat Pack* (1998)
Bruce Greenwood –*Thirteen Days* (2000)

Hal Holbrook played future president **John Adams** in the film *George Washington* (1984). He also played **Abraham Lincoln** in *North and South I* and *II* (1985 and 1986).

Franklin Roosevelt
Jack Young – *Yankee Doodle Dandy* (1942)
Ralph Bellamy – *Sunrise At Campobello* (1960), *The Winds Of War* (1983) and *War And Remembrance* (1988)
Robert Boyd – *Ragtime* (1981)

Ian Wolfe was **Calvin Coolidge** in *Court Martial Of Billy Mitchell* (1955).

John Roarke was **George Bush** in *Naked Gun 2¹/₂: The Smell Of Fear* (1991).

Barry Bostwick played **George Washington** in *George Washington* (1984).

Tom Howard played future President **Lyndon Johnson** in the film *JFK* (1991).

Nick Nolte played **Thomas Jefferson** in *Jefferson In Paris* (1995) and Herbert Heyes played him in *Far Horizons* (1955).

Van Heflin was **Andrew Johnson** in *Tennessee Johnson* (1942).

Alexander Knox played **Woodrow Wilson** in *Wilson* (1944), which won five Oscars and was nominated for best picture.

Charlton Heston played **Andrew Jackson** in *The President's Lady* (1953).

Dwight Eisenhower has been played by Robert Beer in *The Right Stuff* (1983) and Curtis Keene in *IQ* (1994).

Ulysses Grant has been played by Reginald Sheffield in *Centennial Summer* (1946), Joe Crehan in *Silver River* (1947) and Jason Robards in *Legend Of The Lone Ranger* (1981).

Burgess Meredith was **James Madison** in *Magnificent Doll* (1946).

Anthony Hopkins played **Richard Nixon** in *Nixon* (1995) and Dan Hedaya took the role in *Dick* (1999).

In *Amistad* (1997), Nigel Hawthorne was **Martin Van Buren** and Anthony Hopkins played **John Adams**.

PLACE YOUR BETS

According to the American Gaming Association, the gross mainland gambling revenue (the amount wagered, minus winnings) more than trebled between 1991 and 2001, from $8.6 billion (£5.2 billion) to $27.2 billion (£16.4 billion). The country has an estimated 5.3 million gambling addicts, but academics urge caution when linking problem-gambling to availability of outlets. One study, for example, has shown that Nevada has among the lowest rates of adolescent problem-gambling of any state, even though it has by far the most casinos.

Even so, it's understandable that the industry wants to insure itself against the social liberals and religious right-wingers whose unlikely alliance seeks to restrict outlets. During the 1997–8 US Presidential election cycle, gambling businesses dropped over $3 million (£1.8 million) into Republican Party coffers and slipped just under $2 million (£1.2 million) to the Democrats. In fact, the Democratic Party handout was greater than it received from most other commercial lobbyists – namely alcohol ($1 million/$600,000), tobacco ($900,000/£540,000), agribusiness ($1million/£620,000), oil and gas ($1.7 million/£1 million) and chemicals. ($500,000/£300,000). The insurance industry did pay more – around $3 million (£1.8 million) – but, hey, it *knows* how expensive insurance is these days. The Republicans got most of their fighting fund from the insurance ($8 million/£4.8 million), oil and gas ($6 million/£3.6 million), tobacco ($4 million/£2.4 million) and chemicals ($1.7 million/£1 million) sectors.

NAKED AMBITION

American nudists have created a $465 million (£280 million) tourist industry with more than 100 clothes-free 'family centers' opening in the last decade alone. An estimated five million Americans are now devotees (supermodel Elle Macpherson is among the more high-profile), and in California they even have a dedicated footbridge, inevitably nicknamed the Bridge Of Thighs. This links the former Palm Springs estates of Doris Day and Errol Flynn, both now part of the upmarket Desert Shadows nude resort. There's just one problem: on a hot day the metal bridge gets barefoot walkers hopping, and resort managers advise their clients to at least wear sandals. Purists have refused on the grounds that it's wimpy.

LUNAR LEAVES

A sycamore tree flourishing in Washington Square, Philadelphia, was grown from seeds carried to the moon and back by astronaut Stuart Roosa on Apollo 14.

TURNING A DEAF EAR

In Denver, Colorado, Della Drimland filed for divorce after finding out that her husband of seven years was only pretending that he was deaf. Court papers revealed that husband Bill admitted to faking hearing loss. His intention was to escape her nagging.

THE SHRINERS

The Shriners are an American fraternity founded in 1872 by 13 men from the Masonic Order. There are 191 chapters across America and they run 22 hospitals. Known also for their colourful parades, circuses and clowns, the Shriners wear a red fez on official business in the manner of British comedian Tommy Cooper!

IT PAYS TO ADVERTISE

The longest-established advertising company in the United States began life as NW Ayer & Son in 1869 and prospered in Philadelphia in art deco offices on Washington Square. In 1973, it switched locations to New York, where it is today known as NW Ayer ABH International.

'DO AS I SAY, NOT AS I DO'

Although he campaigned on a platform of family values, Ronald Reagan was the only US president to have been divorced.

A PLACE TO HIDE

One of Napoleon's 26 marshals went into self-imposed exile in Philadelphia after failing to turn up for the pivotal Battle of Waterloo. General Count Groucy stayed away from the 1815 confrontation that ended in British and Prussian victory and Napoleon's abdication. While Napoleon spent the rest of his days in isolation on St Helena, his absent general was forced out of France (where public feeling against him was running high) and across the Atlantic.

CABLE NEWS

The first transoceanic cable was received on 16 August 1858 and read: 'Europe and America are united by telegraph. Glory to God in the highest and on earth peace and goodwill to all men.'

HISTORIC HOME

When Jacqueline Kennedy moved into the White House in 1960, she brought through the doors an armchair used by Washington (the first president in the first presidential mansion), third president Thomas Jefferson's inkwell, 12th president Zachary Taylor's fireplace fender, and 21st president Chester Alan Arthur's gold whistle.

HEARING VOICES

Dan Castellaneta not only provides the voice for Homer Simpson in *The Simpsons* but also Grampa Abraham Simpson, big-drinking Barney, Krusty the Clown and Groundskeeper Willie.

Nancy Cartwright does the voice of Bart Simpson but also that of naughty Nelson, Todd Flanders and Ralph Wiggum.

The voice of shopkeeper Apu is that of Hank Azaria, who 'is' also bartender Moe and Chief Wiggum.

Yeardley Smith is the voice of Lisa Simpson.

RIDING HIGH

George Ferris unveiled his new ride for fairground thrill seekers – a giant, steam-driven rotating wheel – at the 1893 World's Fair held in Chicago.

SOUNDS FAMILIAR

Alaska's sombre state song, starting with the words 'Alaska, my Alaska', shares a tune with the festive carol 'Oh, Christmas Tree', which is also used by Britain's Labour Party when members sing 'The Red Flag'. The same tune is used for the Maryland State song, which begins – surprise, surprise – 'Maryland, my Maryland'.

THE POWER OF FLATTERY

Shrewd residents of North Dakota who split from neighbour South Dakota in 1889 named their capital city Bismarck for Prussia's Iron Chancellor Otto von Bismarck. They hoped to attract German investment to the area.

BORN TO RULE

Future President Calvin Coolidge was born on 4 July 1872 in a store in Plymouth, Vermont. It is still open for business today.

SHORT STATE

The only American state with a one-syllable name is Maine.

INSECT TRIBUTE

In Enterprise, Alabama, there stands a fine statue dedicated to the boll weevil, a cotton-eating critter originally from Mexico.

FLYING HIGH

America's first manned balloon flight took place in 1793, when pilot Jean Pierre Blanchard went aloft from an unorthodox launch pad – Walnut Street Jail in Philadelphia. The balloon travelled as far as Gloucester, New Jersey, before bumping back down to earth. President George Washington was among those watching the triumph.

COSTLY CUPPA

During the 'Boston Tea Party', a protest by Americans against colonial rule during 1773, the contents of 342 crates of fine-leaf tea were tipped into harbour waters. Its value at the time was in the region of $29,000 (£18,000).

BIRTH RIGHT

No fewer than eight US heads of state were born in Virginia – the most in any state – so giving the state the nickname 'Mother of Presidents'.

TWICE AS GOOD

New York is popularly thought of as the city that's 'so nice they named it twice'. In fact, the accolade really belongs to the city of Walla Walla (Washington), which takes its name from the Indian for 'many waters'.

PLANETARY PRAISE

Visitors to Florida frequently claim it is out of this world. With towns in the state named Jupiter, Mars, Venus and Neptune, we're inclined to believe them!

CITY AKA'S

'The Big Apple', 'The City of Brotherly Shove' – New York
'Mile High City' – Denver
'Motown' – Detroit (as in 'motor town', for its car manufacturing)
'The City that Care Forgot', 'The Big Easy' – New Orleans
'Smoky City' – Pittsburgh
'Beantown' – Boston (for Boston baked beans)
'Soybean Capital of the World' – Decatur, Illinois
'Second City', 'Windy City' – Chicago
'Porkopolis' – Cincinnati (once famous as pork packing centre)

GENERAL WORDSMITH

George S Patton was one of the toughest generals of World War II, famous for relishing conflict and all it entailed. Yet the granite man, who was an Olympic pentathlete in 1912, pursued the most unlikely hobby – writing poetry.

BAD NEIGHBOURS

Abraham Lincoln and Jefferson Davis, the presidents of the Union and the Confederacy, respectively, during the Civil War, were both born in Kentucky.

SEEING IS BELIEVING

'No one wants to see a man fall 100ft [30m] to his death. But they do want to be there when it happens.'
Harry Houdini

LOST CHILD

Virginia Dare, granddaughter of pioneering Governor John White, was the first child born of English parents in the New World. Her mother was Elenora (née White) and her father was Ananias Dare, one of the governor's assistants. She was born on 18 August 1587, just days after the colonists' arrival on Roanoke Island, North Carolina, and her baptism was the second recorded Christian sacrament administered in North America. (The first had been administered a few days earlier to Manteo, an Indian chief.) Virginia was less than a month old when Governor White was forced to return to England for supplies. (She was one of 114 left behind.) A secret code had been worked out that, should they leave Roanoke Island, they were to carve their new location on a conspicuous tree or post. If the move had to be made because of an attack (either by Indians or Spaniards), they were to carve over the letters or name a distress signal in the form of a Maltese cross. White was delayed by England's tussle with Spain, and three years later he returned to find the word 'Croatoan', without any cross or other sign of distress. To this day, no one is certain where the residents of the lost colony went, or what happened to them.

WAR STORIES

Private Jessica Lynch, the military supply clerk captured by Iraqis during the second Gulf War and rescued by US commandos, returned home to a $1 million (£600,000) book contract. The deal was particularly lucrative, given that she initially claimed to have no memory of what happened.

UNUSUAL UTTERANCES BY FORMER VICE PRESIDENT DAN QUAYLE

'It isn't pollution that's harming the environment. It's the impurities in our air and water that are doing it.'

'This election is about who's going to be the next President of the United States! *2 September 1988, reported in* Esquire, *August 1992*

'If we do not succeed, then we run the risk of failure.'
To the Phoenix Republican Forum, 23 March 1990

'What a waste it is to lose one's mind. Or not to have a mind is being very wasteful. How true that is.' *Winning friends while speaking to the United Negro College Fund, 9 May 1989, reported in the* New York Times, *9 December 1992*

'Republicans understand the importance of bondage between a mother and child.' US News & World Report, *10 October 1988*

'Welcome to President Bush, Mrs. Bush, and my fellow astronauts.' *Addressing the 20th anniversary celebration of the moon landing, 20 July 1989, reported in* Esquire, *August 1992*

'I love California, I practically grew up in Phoenix.'

'We don't want to go back to tomorrow, we want to go forward.'

IT'S THE ECONOMY, STUPID...

Democrat presidents are supposed to spend tax money. Republicans love State prudence. So just how did George W Bush turn an annual US budget surplus of $167 billion (£100 billion) into an annual deficit of $400 billion (£240 billion) within two years of coming to power in 2001? Long-term projections look even grimmer. When Bill 'it's the economy, stupid' Clinton left the White House, America was heading for a $2.9 trillion (£1.75 trillion) budget *surplus* in 2008. By the summer of 2003, this had been revised to a $1.9 trillion (£1.1 trillion) debt. However you dress things up, the American taxpayer is facing an unforeseen $4.9 trillion (£2.9 trillion) bill. Which butthead gave George the mail-order catalogue?

STANDING ALONE

For a while Vermont was a proud republic, after its declaration of independence on 8 July 1777. It wasn't until Vermont officially joined the United States of America in 1791 that the short-lived flirtation with nationhood came to an end.

ICE HOCKEY PLAYER POSITIONS

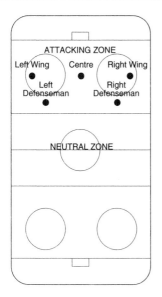
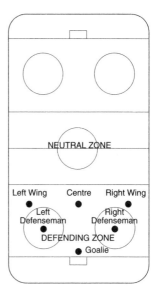

POACHED CHEF

When President George W Bush's head chef, Walter Scheib, was approached to switch jobs and cook for French president Jacques Chirac in August 2003, it seemed like a tantalising career move…especially when the invitation was made verbally by Monsieur Chirac's wife, Bernadette, who told how her husband was sick of Gallic grub and longed for traditional American burgers. The catch? It was all a prank by a French TV show. 'Bernadette' was a lookalike and her 'secretary' was a producer wired with hidden cameras. Fortunately, Walter was tipped off after 20 minutes by staff at his Plaza Athenée hotel in Paris. He went unpoached.

QUITE WHITE

Theodore Roosevelt was the first to coin the phrase 'White House' for the presidential accommodation. Prior to him, the place was called either the President's House or the Executive Mansion.

MEAN WEATHER

Most windy US cities based on average wind speed in kph (mph)

Mount Washington, New Hampshire	57.4 (35.3)
St Paul Island, Alaska	27.3 (17.4)
Cold Bay, Alaska	27.5 (16.9)
Blue Hill, Massachusetts	25.0 (15.4)

Least windy US cities based on average wind speed in kph (mph)

Oak Ridge, Tennessee	7.2 (4.4)
Medford, Oregon	7.8 (4.8)
Talkeetna, Alaska	8.0 (4.9)
McGrath, Alaska	8.5 (5.2)

Maximum recorded US wind speeds in kph (mph)

Mount Washington, New Hampshire	375 (231)
Atlantic City, New Jersey	260 (160)
Raleigh, North Carolina	249 (153)
Valdez, Alaska	153 (94)
Blue Hill, Massachusetts	150 (92)
Fort Myers, Florida	150 (92)

Snowiest US cities based on average snowfall in m (in)

Stampede Pass, Washington	11.19 (440.3)
Valdez, Alaska	8.28 (325.8)
Mount Washington, New Hampshire	6.45 (253.9)

Coldest US cities based on normal minimum in °C (°F)

Barrow, Alaska	-15.5 (4.1)
Barter Island, Alaska	-15.4 (4.3)
Bettles, Alaska	-10.6 (12.9)
Kotzebue, Alaska	-9.3 (15.3)
Mount Washington, New Hampshire	-6.8 (19.8)

Coldest US cities based on record temperatures in °C (°F)

McGrath, Alaska	-59 (-75)
Bettles, Alaska	-57 (-70)
Fairbanks, Alaska	-52 (-62)
Barrow, Alaska	-49 (-56)
Nome, Alaska	-48 (-54)
Williston, North Dakota	-46 (-50)
Glasgow, Montana	-44 (-47)
Mount Washington, New Hampshire	-44 (-47)
Boca, California	-43 (-45)

Hottest US cities based on normal daily maximum in °C (°F)

Yuma, Arizona	31.1 (87.9)
Phoenix, Arizona	29.9 (85.9)
Honolulu, Hawaii	29.1 (84.4)
Kahului, Hawaii	28.3 (83.9)
Fort Myers, Florida	28.3 (83.9)

Hottest US cities based on record temperatures in °C (°F)

Yuma, Arizona	51.1 (124)
Phoenix, Arizona	50.0 (122)
Redding, California	47.8 (118)
Midland-Odessa, Texas	46.7 (116)
Medford, Oregon	46.1 (115)
Lewiston, Idaho	46.1 (115)
Sacramento, California	46.1 (115)

Most number of rainy days

Hilo, Hawaii	278
Yakutat, Alaska	235
Cold Bay, Alaska	226
Annette, Alaska	223
Juneau, Alaska	222
Mount Washington, New Hampshire	209
Quillayute, Washington	208

Cities with the most annual rainfall in m (in)

Yakutat, Alaska	3.84 (151.25)
Hilo, Hawaii	3.28 (129.19)
Quillayute, Washington	2.67 (105.18)
Annette, Alaska	2.62 (103.28)

BARGAIN HUNTER

When Dutchman Peter Minuit bought Manhattan Island from the Man-a-hat-a Indians back in 1626, he did so with $24 (£15) worth of beads and trinkets.

LAW AND DISORDER

Although its crime rate is one of the worst in the US, Miami possesses the American Police Hall of Fame and Museum, dedicated to law enforcement.

BUILDING BLOCKS

- There is a house in Rockport built entirely of newspaper.

- Louisiana has the tallest State Capitol Building in the United States – 137m (450ft) tall, over 34 floors.

- The Chicago post office at 433 West Van Buren is the only postal facility in the world you can drive a car through.

- The amount of copper on the roof of the Capitol Building in Phoenix, Arizona, is equivalent to 4,800,000 pennies.

- The 19 chandeliers in the Capitol in Lansing, Michigan, are like no others and were designed especially for the building by Tiffany's of New York. Weighing between 360kg (800lb) and 410kg (900lb) apiece, they are composed of copper, iron and pewter.

- The name of the red marble that gives its colour to the Colorado State Capitol is Beulah Red. Don't even think about trying to emulate the effect at home, however, as all the Beulah Red marble in the world went into building the Capitol.

- Iolani Palace, Hawaii, is the only royal palace in the United States.

- The world's first skyscraper was built in Chicago in 1885.

- The Memorial Bell Tower at Cathedral of the Pines in Rindge, New Hampshire, has four bronze bas-reliefs designed by Norman Rockwell. The bell tower is specifically dedicated to women — military and civilian — who died serving their country.

- Dubuque, Iowa, is home to the only county courthouse with a gold dome.

- The Cathedral Basilica of the Assumption in Covington, Kentucky, has 82 stained-glass windows, including the world's largest hand-blown one. The window measures 7.3m (24ft) wide by 20.5m (67ft) high and depicts the Council of Ephesus with 134 life-sized figures.

THE PENTAGON

Home to the Department of Defense, its architect was George Bergstrom and its location is Arlington, Virginia (near Washington, DC). Constructed between 1941 and 1943, the building is made with reinforced concrete outer walls, wood framing and a slate roof in neoclassical style. With 13.8 hectares (34 acres) of space in five concentric rings, the Pentagon is considered the largest office building in the world. Brigadier General

Brehon B Somervell became the prime planner for the Pentagon in 1941. He and his associates took less than four days to develop plans for a three-storey building to house 40,000 people. Immediately after the Pearl Harbour attack, a fourth floor was added to the plan, and later a fifth. To conserve steel and other metals, concrete ramps instead of elevators were used to connect the floors, and the outside walls were made of reinforced concrete. About eight months after beginning, the contractor completed the first two sections of the building and War Department personnel began to move in. The building was finished by 15 January 1943. It was badly damaged by the impact of a hijacked 757 jet aeroplane on 11 September 2001 at 9:43am, in the same series of attacks that destroyed the World Trade Center in New York.

- It is 24m (71ft) high, five storeys tall, plus it has a mezzanine and basement.

- The five concentric rings are named A, B, C, D and E, from the inner ring facing the courtyard (A ring) to the outside ring (E).

- It measures 321m (921ft) along each outer-side façade.

- Of its 600,000 sq m (6.5 million square ft) floor area, 340,000 sq m (3.7 million square ft) are used for offices.

- Construction cost $80 million (£48 million) – in 1943 dollars!

- The building has 28km (17.5 miles) of corridors.

- Up to 13,000 workers were employed in its construction. Around 4,500,000 cubic m (6,000,000 cubic yd) of earth were moved, and 41,492 concrete pilings were driven. The construction documents included 2,500 sheets of drawings, typically sized 86 x 152cm (34 x 60in), and 310,000 cubic m (410,000 cubic yd) of concrete went into the building, using 620,000 tonnes (680,000 tons) of sand and gravel dredged from the adjacent Potomac River.

MALE CHAUVINISTS BEWARE!

To the uninitiated, the state flag of Virginia shows a woman crushing a man underfoot. In fact, it is the depiction of an Amazonian warrior trampling a tyrant underfoot and bears the motto *Sic semper tyrannis* ('Thus always to tyrants'). Spookily, it was this very phrase that John Wilkes Booth uttered (in Latin) upon shooting Abraham Lincoln.

KEY PRESIDENTIAL INAUGURATIONS

George Washington – 30 April 1789
- Oath of office taken out of doors (balcony of Federal Hall in New York City).
- Pronounced the words 'So help me God' after taking the oath. Other presidents have followed this example.
- Set the precedent of kissing the Bible after the oath.

George Washington – 4 March 1793
- Shortest inaugural address (135 words).

Thomas Jefferson – 4 March 1801
- Began the custom of writing to Congress to accept the inauguration and arrange the time for the ceremonies.
- First president to be inaugurated at the Capitol in Washington, DC (in the Senate Chamber).

John Quincy Adams – 4 March 1825
- First president to be sworn in wearing long trousers.

Martin Van Buren – 4 March 1837
- First time the outgoing and incoming presidents (Jackson and Van Buren) rode together in a carriage to the Capitol for the inaugural.
- First use of inaugural programmes.
- First use of floats in an inaugural parade.
- First time two inaugural balls were held.

John Tyler – 6 April 1841
- First vice president to assume the presidency due to the death of the president.

James Polk – 4 March 1845
- First inauguration to be covered by telegraph.
- First known newspaper illustration of a presidential inauguration (*Illustrated London News*).

Franklin Pierce – 4 March 1853
- Drove to and from the Capitol standing up in his carriage.
- Affirmed (rather than swore) the oath of office.
- Broke precedent by not kissing the Bible, but merely placing his left hand on it.
- First president to deliver inaugural address without referring to notes.

Rutherford Hayes – 3 March 1877 and 5 March 1877
- First president to take the oath of office in the White House.
- Sworn in prior to Inauguration Day, because it fell on Sunday. Took oath privately on Saturday 3 March, then publicly on the following Monday.

Theodore Roosevelt – 4 September 1901

- The only president not sworn in on a Bible. Mr Ansley Wilcox, at whose home Roosevelt took the oath of office, wrote in 1903, 'According to my best recollection no Bible was used, but President Roosevelt was sworn in with uplifted hand.'

Franklin Roosevelt – 20 January 1937

- First president to be inaugurated on the 20 January date, a change made by the 20th Amendment to the Constitution.

Franklin Roosevelt – 10 January 1945

- First and only time a president was inaugurated for a fourth term. (The 22nd Amendment to the Constitution, ratified in 1951, restricts the presidency to two terms.)

Dwight Eisenhower – 20 January 1953

- Broke with custom by reciting his own improvised prayer instead of kissing the Bible.

John F Kennedy – 20 January 1961

- First time a poet, Robert Frost, participated in the official ceremonies at the Capitol
- As the first Catholic elected president, Kennedy was the first to use a Catholic (Douay) version of the Bible for his oath.
- Last president to wear traditional stovepipe hat to the inauguration.

Lyndon Johnson – 22 November 1963

- First time the oath was administered in an aeroplane (Air Force One, a Boeing 707, at Love Field in Dallas, Texas).
- First time the oath was administered by a woman – Sarah T Hughes, US District Judge of the Northern District of Texas.

Gerald Ford – 4 August 1974

- First unelected vice president to assume the presidency.
- First vice president to assume the presidency under the provisions of the 25th Amendment to the Constitution, which specifies that, on the resignation of the president, the vice president shall become president (in this case, Richard Nixon).

Bill Clinton – 20 January 1997

- First time the ceremony was broadcast live on the Internet.

George W Bush – 20 January 2001

- First time a former president (George HW Bush) attended his son's inauguration as president.

SAME NAME

When Franklin Roosevelt married his wife Eleanor, she did not have to change her signature. As his cousin she was already a Roosevelt and, in fact, became Eleanor Roosevelt Roosevelt.

HIDDEN HISTORY

In 1995 when the US Postal Service realised it couldn't get all the necessary information condensed to the size of a postage stamp, it had the problem licked by putting descriptions of the Civil War events being commemorated on the back of the stamps.

AMISH BELIEFS

Although the Amish are said to inhabit 'Dutch' country in Pennsylvania, their ancestors actually came from Switzerland in the early 1700s after being persecuted for possessing Anabaptist beliefs. Today, the Amish live simply in self-imposed seclusion, dress in uniformly plain clothes and reject modern technology (including cars and zips!).

FOR WHOM THE BELL TOLLS

The Liberty Bell, tolled at the first public reading of the Declaration of Independence, was in fact made in London, capital of the colonialists. Later, abolitionists adopted the bell as a symbol of freedom thanks to its biblical inscription that reads: 'Proclaim liberty through all the land, to all the inhabitants thereof' (Leviticus 25:10). After 1846, it could no longer be used, having cracked. It was moved to its present site in Philadelphia in 1976.

BLUE IS GREEN

Although Kentucky is known as the Bluegrass State, it is more green than blue. That's because the blue flower that gives Kentucky its nickname is swiftly munched by grazing animals, which leave just the foliage behind, in a common or garden shade of green.

WHAT'S IN A NAME?

The Badlands of South Dakota won the name from a translation of the Native American term, *mako sica*.

LONE VOICE

Jeanette Rankin, the first woman elected to the US House of Representatives in 1916, was the only member of Congress to oppose the declaration of war on Japan in 1941 following Pearl Harbour. 'Killing more people won't help matters,' she explained.

PRESIDENTS APPEARING ON MOUNT RUSHMORE

George Washington (far left) – completed 1930
Thomas Jefferson (centre left) – completed 1936
Abraham Lincoln (far right) – completed 1937
Theodore Roosevelt (centre right) – completed 1939

The creator of the 18m (60ft) faces was sculptor Gutzon Borglum, who led a dedicated team until his death in March 1941. Borglum also created a mighty 42-figure bronze sculpture in Newark, New Jersey, called *The Wars Of America*.

PASSING GO

When Monopoly was launched in America in the summer of 1935, it sold at a rate of 20,000 boards a week.

STATE NICKNAMES AND MOTTOS

State	Nickname	Motto
Alabama	Cotton State	*Audemus jura nostra defendere* (We dare defend our rights)
Alaska	The Last Frontier Land of the Midnight Sun The Great Land	North to the future
Arizona	Grand Canyon State	*Ditat Deus* (God enriches)
Arkansas	Land of Opportunity Natural State Wonder State	*Regnat populus* (The people rule)
California	Golden State	*Eureka* (I have found it)
Colorado	Centennial State	*Nil sine numine* (Nothing without providence)
Connecticut	Constitution State	*Qui transtulit sustinet* (He who transplanted still sustains)
Delaware	Diamond State First State	Liberty and independence
Florida	Sunshine State Peninsula State	In God we trust
Georgia	Peach State Empire of the South	Wisdom, justice and moderation
Hawaii	Aloha State Paradise of the Pacific	*Ua mau ke ea o ka aina I ka pono* (The life of the land is perpetuated in righteousness)
Idaho	Gem State	*Esto perpetua* (Let it be perpetual/It is for ever)
Illinois	Land of Lincoln National Union Prairie State	State sovereignty, national union
Indiana	Hoosier State	The crossroads of America

Iowa	Hawkeye State Corn State	Our liberties we prize and our rights we will maintain
Kansas	Sunflower State Jayhawker State	*Ad astra per aspera* (To the stars through difficulties)
Kentucky	Bluegrass State	United we stand, divided we fall
Louisiana	Pelican State Creole State Sugar State	Union, justice and confidence
Maine	Pine Tree State	*Dirigo* (I direct)
Maryland	Old Line State Free State	*Fatti maschil parole femine* (Manly deeds, womanly words)
Massachusetts	Bay State Old Colony State	*Ense petit placidam sub libertate quietem* (By the sword we seek peace, but peace only under liberty)
Michigan	Wolverine State Water Wonderland Great Lakes State	*Si quaeris peninsulam amoenam, circumspice* (If you seek a pleasant peninsula, look about you)
Minnesota	North Star State Gopher State Land of 10,000 Lakes	*L'Etoile du nord* (The star of the north)
Mississippi	Magnolia State	*Virtute et armis* (By valour and arms)
Missouri	Show me State	Salus populi suprema lex esto (The welfare of the people shall be the supreme law)
Montana	Treasure State Big Sky Country	*Oro y plata* (Gold and silver)
Nebraska	Beef State Cornhusker State	Equality before the law
Nevada	Silver State Sagebrush State Battle Born State	All for our country

STATE NICKNAMES AND MOTTOS (CONT'D)

State	Nickname	Motto
New Hampshire	Granite State	Live free or die
New Jersey	Garden State	Liberty and prosperity
New Mexico	Land of Enchantment Sunshine State	*Crescit eundo* (It grows as it goes)
New York	Excelsior State Empire State	*Excelsior* (Higher)
North Carolina	Tar Heel State Old North State	*Esse quam videri* (To be, rather than to seem)
North Dakota	Flickertail State Sioux State Peace Garden State	Liberty and union, now and for ever, one and inseparable
Ohio	Buckeye State	With God, all things are possible
Oklahoma	Sooner State	*Labor omnia vincit* (Labour conquers all things)
Oregon	Beaver State	*Alis volat propiis* (She flies with her own wings)
Pennsylvania	Keystone State	Virtue, liberty and independence
Rhode Island	Little Rhody Ocean State Plantation State	Hope
South Carolina	Palmetto State	Prepared in mind and resources/While I breathe, I hope
South Dakota	Mt Rushmore State Coyote State Sunshine State	Under God the people rule
Tennessee	Volunteer State	Agriculture and commerce
Texas	Lone Star State	Friendship
Utah	Beehive State	Industry
Vermont	Green Mountain State	Freedom and unity

Virginia	Old Dominion State	*Sic semper tyrannis*
	Mother of Presidents	(Thus always to tyrants)
Washington	Evergreen State	*Alki* (By and by)
West Virginia	Mountain State	*Montani semper liberi*
		(Mountaineers are always free)
Wisconsin	Badger State	Forward
	America's Dairyland	
Wyoming	Equality State	Equal rights
	Cowboy State	

SACRED ICON

The dramatic landscape which drew aliens to earth in Steven Spielberg's 1977 film *Close Encounters Of The Third Kind* is in fact a national monument called the Devil's Tower. Sacred to 23 Native American tribes, this volcanic residue dates back millions of years and was once described, by a Lakota leader, as 'the heart of everything that is'.

SPACE DUST

In 1992, the ashes of Gene Roddenberry, creator of *Star Trek*, were scattered beyond the final frontier after being transported to the stars by the space shuttle *Columbia*.

MONEY TALKS

In December 1927, J Edgar Hoover, in his capacity as commerce secretary, announced that the average annual salary in the US was $1,280 (£260).

THE 'STAR SPANGLED BANNER'...

...became the official US anthem from 3 March 1931.

JOKE STATE MOTTOS

Alabama	At least we're not Mississippi
Alaska	11,623 Eskimos can't be wrong!
Arizona	Dehyd-rific!
Arkansas	Litterasy ain't everthing
California	As seen on TV
Colorado	If you don't ski, don't bother
Connecticut	Like Massachusetts, only dirtier and with less character
Delaware	Is Delaware a state?
Florida	Ask us about our grandkids
Georgia	We put the 'fun' in fundamentalist extremism
Hawaii	*Haka tiki mou sha'ami* (meaning 'Death to mainland scum, but leave your money')
Idaho	More than just potatoes... Well, OK, we're not, but the potatoes sure are real good
Illinois	Gateway to Iowa
Indiana	Two billion years tidal wave free
Iowa	Land of James T Kirk
Kansas	Don't blame us, we voted for Dole
Kentucky	Five million people, fifteen last names
Louisiana	We're not all drunken Cajun wackos, but that's our tourism campaign
Maine	Cheap lobster
Maryland	A thinking man's Delaware
Massachusetts	Our taxes are lower than Sweden's (for most tax brackets)
Michigan	First line of defense from the Canadians
Minnesota	Land of 7,000 lakes and 3,000 man-made ponds
Mississippi	Come feel better about your own state
Missouri	Your federal flood relief tax dollars at work
Montana	Land of the big sky, the unabomer, and very little else
Nebraska	Ask about our state motto contest
Nevada	Whores and poker!
New Hampshire	Go away and leave us alone
New Jersey	The garbage state
New Mexico	Lizards make excellent pets
New York	You have the right to remain silent, you have the right to an attorney
North Carolina	Tobacco is a vegetable
North Dakota	Um... We've got... um... dinosaur bones? Yeah, dinosaur bones!

Ohio	Don't judge us by Cleveland
Oklahoma	Like the play, only no singing
Oregon	Spotted owl, it's what's for dinner
Pennsylvania	Cook with coal
Rhode Island	We're not *really* an island
South Carolina	Remember the Civil War? We didn't actually surrender
South Dakota	Closer than North Dakota
Tennessee	The educashun state
Texas	*Se hablo ingles*
Utah	Our Jesus is better than your Jesus
Vermont	Yep
Virginia	Who says Government stiffs and slackjaw yokels don't mix?
Washington	Help! We're overrun by nerds and slackers!
West Virginia	One big happy family – really!
Wisconsin	Come cut our cheese
Wyoming	Why are you here?

BILL AND HILL

Former First Lady Hillary Rodham Clinton got a £5 million ($8 million) advance for her book *Living History*, a tome which includes curtain-twitching bedside scenes of President Bill confessing his adultery. Public humiliation aside, the Clintons have done all right since they left the White House. The 'Bill and Hill' show – their combined private earnings – apparently topped £22 million ($37 million) in 2002.

KILLING FIELDS

In 1928 – the year that 'Ol' Man River' was a worldwide hit – nine blacks were lynched by mobs. This was the lowest figure in 40 years.

SMILE FOR NYLON

The first nylon-based products to go on sale in America were toothbrushes, which hit the shelves in New Jersey in February 1938. Nylon stockings became available in America a year later, at a cost of $1.15 (70p) a pair.

LIGHTS OUT

Henry Ford, creator of the mass-produced car, died by candlelight in April 1947 at the age of 83. Floods in his home city of Detroit had caused power cuts.

BEST RED PAPER

The *Daily Worker*, America's last remaining Communist newspaper, was published for the last time in January 1958.

TREATIES OR AGREEMENTS THAT INCREASED THE SIZE OF THE UNITED STATES

1. Treaty of Paris, 1783
2. Louisiana Purchase, 1803
3. West Florida annexation, 1810
4. Treaty of Ghent, 1814
5. Convention of 1818
6. Oregon Treaty, 1846
7. Treaty of Guadeloupe Hidalgo, 1848
8. Gadsden Purchase, 1853
9. Alaska Purchase, 1867
10. Hawaii annexation, 1898

A–Z OF WORDS EVERY US HIGH-SCHOOL STUDENT SHOULD KNOW AND UNDERSTAND*

Abstemious	Jejune	Soliloquy
Bowdlerize	Kinetic	Tautology
Churlish	Loquacious	Unctuous
Deleterious	Moiety	Vehement
Enfranchise	Nanotechnology	Winnow
Fatuous	Oligarchy	Xenophobe
Gamete	Plagiarize	Yeoman
Hegemony	Quotidian	Ziggurat
Irony	Reciprocal	

*According to the editors of American Heritage Dictionaries

STRONG STUFF

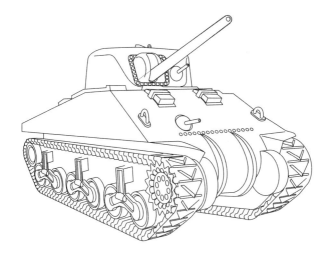

America's Sherman tank, named after US Civil War General William Tecumseh Sherman, was the one most frequently used by the Americans and British during World War II. The first one rolled off the production line in 1942, and was capable of covering a distance of around 232km (145 miles) at a speed of about 40kph (25mph). In total, 41,530 were made before the end of hostilities in 1945.

STREET OF FAME

Laramie Street, the legendary Hollywood film set used for Warner Brothers Westerns since 1930, was bulldozed in 2003 to make way for a development of 11 luxury New England-style clapboard homes. Studio bosses say the Western is passé. Here are six of the best from Laramie's golden years, together with their star names:

Blazing Saddles (Gene Wilder)
Cheyenne Autumn (Richard Widmark and James Stewart)
Dodge City (Errol Flynn)
The Good Guys And The Bad Guys (Robert Mitchum)
The Left Handed Gun (Paul Newman)
Wells Fargo (Joel McCrea)

VEGGY GOOD

In Wilton, Maine there's a cannery that imports and cans only dandelion greens.

Clark is known as the potato capital of South Dakota, and is home to the 'world-famous' Mashed Potato Wrestling contest.

Castroville, California, is known as the artichoke capital of the world. The very first young woman to be crowned 'Artichoke Queen' was Norma Jean Baker – later known as Marilyn Monroe.

In 1976 Jim Ellis of Montrose, Michigan, set the world record for grape eating after he consumed 1.4kg (3lb 1oz) in 34.6 seconds.

Statistics from the National Onion Association show that American onion consumption has risen by around 50 per cent over the past 20 years.

In New Haven, Connecticut, during colonial times, it was the habit to use a cut pumpkin as a guide to ensure a uniform style for haircuts. This led, unsurprisingly, to the nickname 'pumpkin-heads'.

Hawaii produces more than one-third of the world's commercial supply of pineapples.

KEY CATHOLIC SHRINES

- Our Lady of Guadalupe, Camelback Mountain, Arizona
- Our Lady of Peace, Santa Clara, California
- Our Lady of La Leche, St Augustine, Florida
- Shrine of Milwaukee, Holy Hill, Chicago, Illinois
- Sanctuary of Mary, Monte Casino, Spencer County, Indiana
- Our Lady of Martyrs, Auriesville, upstate New York
- Our Lady of Fatima, Holliston, Massachusetts
- National Sanctuary of Our Sorrowful Mother, Portland, Ohio

WINTER TERROR

In January 1922, 107 people died when the roof of the Knickerbocker Theater, Washington, collapsed under the weight of snow.

LOOKS ILLEGAL

After 21 August 1923, it became illegal for dancing partners to stare in their partner's eyes in the city of Kalamazoo, Michigan.

BODY COUNT

The first American census was taken in 1790 by around 600 US marshals on horseback. In an exercise that lasted 18 months, a total of 3,929,214 inhabitants were counted as living in the infant republic.

THE FIRST TELEVISED DEBATE

This took place between presidential hopefuls, Gerald Ford and Jimmy Carter, in September 1976. Carter won the election two months later.

MILLION-DOLLAR MAN

Before his death in 1921, opera singer Caruso became the first major singer to become a recording artist, notching up 154 recordings and earning royalties of almost $1.6 million (£1 million). Such was his fame and following, he had earned $1,150 (£700) a night appearing at the Metropolitan Opera in New York.

DEATH WATCH

On 3 August 1925, a court in Indiana ruled that a motorist found guilty of killing a pedestrian would be punished by spending one hour alone with the victim's body.

RECORD BREAKER

On 23 April 1921, American Charles Paddock became the world's fastest human when he ran 100m in 10.4 seconds at Redlands, California. He always sought luck by touching wood before he raced, and fostered a distinctive leap for the line at the end of his exertions. Paddock had already set a world record by running 200m in 20.8 seconds on 26 March.

ROYAL WELCOME

A British sovereign welcomed an American president to Britain for the first time in December 1918, following the outbreak of peace in Europe. King George V and his wife Queen Mary met Woodrow Wilson at Charing Cross station and escorted him to Buckingham Palace. Mr Wilson had travelled by ship to Dover, following a triumphal tour of France.

POST COAST TO COAST

A daily east–west airmail service running between San Francisco and New York got off the ground on 6 September 1920.

CHEERS!

- When Prohibition ended in the United States on 5 February 1933, apparently 1.5 million barrels of beer were drunk in a single evening.

- Hawaii is the only state that grows coffee.

- California produces more than 64 million litres (17 million gallons) of wine each year.

- Elijah Craig, a Baptist preacher, was reputedly the first man to have made bourbon whiskey in Scott County, Kentucky, when (in 1789) he stored his wares in barrels that had been charred in a fire. According to federal law, to call itself bourbon it must be 51 per cent corn distilled at less than 160 per cent proof, it must be aged for at least two years in new, charred oak barrels, and it must be made in the USA.

DEATH'S A GAS

America's first gas chamber execution took place on 8 February 1924.

SHARP SHOOTER

On 5 March 1922, Annie Oakley shot a record 98 clay targets out of 100 from a distance of nearly 15m (48ft).

WASTE NOT, WANT NOT

- In 1990, the world's tallest cake – standing at 100 tiers high, and measuring 30.1m (101ft 2½in) – was made by Beth Cornell Trevorrow and friends for the Shiawassee County Fair in Michigan in 1990.

- It has been estimated that if Americans were to reduce the amount of meat that they eat by 10 per cent, the savings in grains and soya beans would be enough to feed 60 million people. This is precisely the number of people who are estimated to starve worldwide each year.

- The average American eats 20 to 30 times as much salt as is required for good health.

- If all the pizza slices Americans eat in one day came from one giant pizza, it would cover more than 11 (American) football fields.

- In October 1995 the fast-food chain Kentucky Fried Chicken was responsible for making the world's largest chicken pie. It measured 3.7m (12ft) across and weighed in at 10,060kg (22,178lb).

- It takes approximately 150 litres (40 gallons) of sap to make approximately 3.8 litres (1 gallon) of maple syrup.

- The average American family of four eats more than 2.2 tonnes (2.5 tons) of food each year.

PRESIDENTIAL NICKNAMES

Teflon man – Ronald Reagan, because no accusations or insinuations seemed to stick to him

Old Hickory – Andrew Jackson, on account of his preference for carrying a cane

Dubya – George W Bush, because of the way southerners pronounce the initial of his middle name

Tricky Dicky – Richard Nixon, following the twists of the Watergate scandal

Father of the Navy – John Adams

The Fugitive President – James Madison (forced to leave Washington in the War of 1812)

Old Man Eloquent – John Quincy Adams

General Mum – William Henry Harrison, because he didn't say much

The Ancient Gorilla – Abraham Lincoln, for appearance's sake

Bulldog – Ulysses Grant

Draft Dodger – Grover Cleveland, with reference to his lack of service in the Civil War

Bull in a China Shop – Theodore Roosevelt

Mr Gloomy Face – Dwight Eisenhower, a name first given to him at West Point

FIRST AMERICAN ACE

The first American to win the men's singles title at Wimbledon was William Tilden, who triumphed over Gerald Patterson in 1920.

BELATED DEMOCRACY

The 19th amendment to the American Constitution, giving women the vote in federal elections, was ratified on 26 August 1920.

SCREAM FOR ICE CREAM

- Apparently Ben and Jerry's ice cream company gives their ice-cream waste to the local Vermont farmers, who use it to feed their hogs. It seems that the hogs like all of the flavours except 'Mint Oreo'.

- Americans eat 3.8 billion litres (almost 1 billion gallons) of ice cream per year. That averages more than 15 litres (4 gallons) per person.

- The ice-cream cone was invented at the St Louis World's Fair in 1904. An ice-cream vendor ran out of cups and asked a waffle vendor to help by rolling up waffles to hold the ice cream.

TEXAS STAR

On 4 November 1924, the first woman state governor, Miriam Ferguson (affectionately known as 'Ma'), was elected in Texas. One of her first acts was to ban the wearing of masks in public – a step designed to curtail the activities of the Ku Klux Klan. Her tenure was short-lived, however, for she resigned in July 1926 after losing primary elections.

VOTE WINNERS

Of the 42 American presidents that have held power, 18 have been Republicans, 14 have been Democrats, 4 have been Whigs, 4 have been Democratic-Republicans (which preceded the Democratic Party) and 2 have been Federalists.

DEATH AND GLORY

John Adams and Thomas Jefferson, the second and third presidents of the USA, both died on 4 July 1826, on the 50th anniversary of American independence.

GIRL POWER

On 6 August 1923, American Henry Sullivan became the third man to swim across the English Channel, in 26 hours and 50 minutes. (The first to achieve the feat, Englishman Matthew Webb, completed the route in 21 hours and 45 minutes on 25 August 1875.) Three years to the day after Sullivan took the plunge, New Yorker Gertrude Ederle, a bronze medallist at the 1925 Paris Olympics, became the first woman to swim the Channel. Her time was 14 hours and 31 minutes.

STICKY PROBLEM

Twenty-one people were killed in 1919 when Boston was flooded with sticky molasses after a 530,000 litre (2 million gallon) storage tank burst.

SPLASH!

When a paddle steamer carrying a circus menagerie was wrecked off the US coast in 1836, a number of sailors clung to a life raft and hoped to be saved. Their chances were dashed, however, when an elephant also trying to save its skin jumped onto the precarious platform. All were drowned.

THANKSGIVING SCRAPS

- Served at the first Thanksgiving meal in 1621 were lobster, roasted pigeon, eel, stuffed cod, turkeys, pumpkins, sweet potatoes, popcorn and cranberry sauce. There were 92 Native Americans at this breakfast.

- More turkeys are raised in California than in any other state in the US.

- The five most popular ways to serve left-over Thanksgiving turkey are: sandwich, soup or stew, casserole, stir-fry and salad.

- When Neil Armstrong and Edwin 'Buzz' Aldrin sat down to eat their first meal on the Moon, their foil food packets contained roasted turkey and all of the trimmings.

MOVING MOMENT

After President Wilson signed the declaration that pitched the USA into World War I on 6 April 1917, he saw cheering crowds in the public galleries of the Senate and the House of Representatives. When he returned to the White House, he remarked, 'My message was one of death for young men. How odd it seems to applaud that.' He then put his heads into his hands and wept.

LONG STRETCH

The longest frontier in the world lies between the USA and Canada, stretching some 6,416km (3,987 miles).

THE BUSINESS OF FOOD

- In 1950, Diner's Club and American Express launched their charge cards in the USA. This was followed in 1951 by the launch of the Diner's Club credit card to 200 customers, which could be used at 27 New York restaurants.

- William Kellogg invented the cornflake in 1906.

- Seattle, Washington, was home to the first revolving restaurant, which opened in 1961.

- The first self-service food store opened in California in 1912.

- The first product to possess a UPC bar code on its packaging was Wrigley's chewing gum.

LATE DATE

Although Independence Day marks the adoption of the Declaration of Independence, which occurred in 1776, it was not legally made into a public holiday until 1941.

BORN TO BET

Americans spend more than £390 billion ($650 billion) annually on legal gambling – more than they do on food. With a further £230 billion ($380 billion) wagered illegally each year on sporting contests, and countless billions staked on backroom card games, this is a nation born to bet!

THE WORLD'S GREATEST SLOT MACHINE CHEAT

This is thought to be Ronald Harris, a crooked employee of the Nevada Gaming Control Board, who (with an accomplice) defied odds of 230,000 to 1 to win $100,000 (£60,000) on an Atlantic City keno (similar to bingo) game. In January 1995, Harris used specialised software on his laptop computer to plug into the machine and predict winning numbers. After the cops caught up with him, he got seven years in jail.

BOOM TOWN

The population of New York had exceeded one million by 1875. It reached the million mark just 65 years after London, but a good 2,000 years after Rome.

WILD ABOUT BILL

'Physically, he was a delight to look upon. Tall, lithe, and free in every motion, he rode and walked as if every muscle was perfection, and the careless swing of his body as he moved seemed perfectly in keeping with the man, the country, the time in which he lived.'

Description of **Wild Bill Hickok** *by Libbie, wife of the ill-fated General Custer*

WEIRD BUT TRUE

- In Gainesville, Georgia – the 'Chicken Capital of the World' – it is illegal to eat chicken with a fork.

- On 13 January 2002, President George W Bush fainted after choking on a pretzel.

- An Idaho law forbids a citizen to give another citizen a box of candy that weighs more than 23kg (50lb).

- Las Cruces, New Mexico, makes the world's largest enchilada. The first weekend in October there is known as the 'Whole Enchilada Fiesta'.

- Less than one-third of the meals eaten in America are served to the whole family at once.

- At one time it was against the law to serve ice cream on cherry pie in Kansas.

- The pecan is the official nut of Alabama.

- Vinita, Oklahoma, hosts an annual 'Calf-Fry Festival' in mid-September. Calf fries are also known as prairie oysters, which are beef testicles – yum yum!

EMBATTLED BREW

Vernor's ginger ale was created in Detroit, and became the first soda pop made in the United States. In 1862, pharmacist James Vernor was trying to create a new drink when he was called away to serve in the Civil War. When he returned, four years later, the drink he had stored in an oak case had acquired a gingery flavour.

TAKEOUT TOPICS

- In 1960, there were 200 calories in a regular portion of McDonald's fries. In 2003, there are 610.

- Rutland, North Dakota, went into *The Guinness Book Of World Records* in 1982, with the cooking and eating of the world's largest hamburger. That year, between 8,000 and 10,000 people came to sample the 1,629kg (3,591lb) burger.

- Des Plaines, Illinois, was home to the first McDonald's.

- In 1934, Carl Kaelen launched the cheeseburger at his burger bar in Louisville, Kentucky.

- The trademark for the name 'cheeseburger' was awarded to Louis Ballast of Denver, Colorado, in 1935.

GOD BLESS AMERICA

A study of 393 cardiac patients at San Francisco General Hospital has produced some scientifically inexplicable results on the power of prayer. Patients were asked if they wanted to take part in the trials, but weren't told whether anyone would actually be praying for them. Half the sample was then prayed for by a group of strangers, who had only their first names. This group of patients needed fewer drugs during convalescence, experienced fewer complications, had a lower risk of pneumonia and was able to leave hospital earlier.

In case you think that praying only works for Americans, researchers at Columbia University in New York persuaded people in Canada, Australia and the US to pray for named women undergoing IVF treatment in Korea. The rates for successful implantation of embryos among the Korean women went up from 8 per cent to 16 per cent. Some experts are now suggesting that prayer groups should be set up in every American hospital.

SWEET COCA-COLA

The world-famous Coca-Cola was invented by Dr John Pemberton in 1886. It has proved remarkably enduring, and millions of dollars have been generated through its worldwide sales.

HIGH-FACTOR SUNCREAM

The physicist Edward Teller, architect of the atomic bomb, had a nicely understated sense of humour. To emphasise his belief in the safety of the bomb's after-effects, he turned up for the first test in New Mexico clutching a bottle of suntan oil. Even so, it must have been a nervy moment. One of Teller's jobs during the wartime Manhattan Project (to build the bomb) was to ensure that, in theory, the explosion wouldn't set fire to the Earth's atmosphere and oceans. He concluded that such an Armageddon was 'unlikely'. Isn't science wonderful?

IN THE BEGINNING

The original 13 states that made up America after Independence were: Connecticut, Massachusetts, Delaware, Georgia, Maryland, Pennsylvania, South Carolina, North Carolina, New York, New Jersey, New Hampshire, Rhode Island and Virginia.

ICE-COOL GRETZKY

It is not for nothing that ice hockey legend Wayne Gretzky was nicknamed 'The Great One'. The Brantford, Ontario-born star holds the NHL (National Hockey League) career record for most points (2,795), goals (885), assists (1,190), number of 100-point-plus seasons (15) and the number of consecutive point-scoring games (51).

COOKIE MONSTROUS

- The Popsicle was invented in 1923 when Frank Epperson left his lemonade mix on the windowsill overnight. They were originally called Epsicles.

- The world's largest cookie and cracker factory, where Nabisco made 16 billion Oreo cookies in 1995, is located in Chicago.

- Between 22 and 26 March 1996, pupils from Pittsville Elementary School, Wisconsin, popped enough corn to fill a box measuring 12m (40ft) long by 2m (6ft 8in) wide, breaking the world record for the most popped corn in a container. They were helped by local residents.

- Fleer's Dubble Bubble was the first bubblegum to go on sale in the United States, in 1928.

- M&M sweets were first launched in military ration packs in 1940.

- Okmulgee holds the world record for largest pecan pie, pecan cookie, pecan brownie, and biggest ice cream and cookie party. Each June, Okmulgee rolls out the welcome mat as the annual Pecan Festival comes to town.

- Twinkies snack cakes were invented in 1930 by James Dewar of the Continental Baking Company in Chicago. Dewar supposedly ate two Twinkies a day until he died in 1985.

CUNNING STUNTS

Silent movie legend Buster Keaton was a superb natural athlete who rarely used a stunt double (one notable exception was the appearance of Olympic pole-vaulter Lee Garmes, who had to vault through a second-storey window on Keaton's behalf). Yet his desire to live the action backfired badly in the film *Sherlock Junior*, in which Keaton is seen running along the top of a locomotive into a waterspout. The force of the water sent him headfirst onto the track, breaking his neck, although there is nothing in the footage to suggest that anything is wrong. Keaton just jumps up and runs away.

SUNDAY, SUNDAE

The ice-cream 'sundae' was named in Evanston, Illinois. The piety of the town resented the dissipating influences of the soda fountain on Sunday, and, yielding to churchly influence, the town fathers passed an ordinance prohibiting the sale of ice-cream sodas on the Lord's day. Ingenious confectioners and drugstore operators obeying the law served ice cream with the syrup of your choice without the soda. Then, objections were made to christening a dish after the Sabbath, so the spelling of 'Sunday' was changed.

WEIRD TALES

Classic characters from *Weird Tales* magazine, undisputed master of American pulp horror between 1923 and 1954:

- Doctor Satan
- The Damp Man
- The Insistent Ghost
- Serpent Princess
- The Whispering Gorilla
- Skull of the Marquis de Sade
- Nursemaid to Nightmares
- Mr Hyde – and Seek
- Mistress Sary
- The Professional Corpse

ROLL OUT THE PORK BARREL

America and free markets go hand in hand – unless, of course, you count farming and imports. George W Bush's 2002 Farm Bill means that US taxpayers will hand out an *extra* $135 billion (£81 billion) in 2004 and 2005 to their farmers, which is the greatest subsidy per head of any country on the planet. America is by no means the only subsidy-hooked Western power, but critics point out that its huge surplus of cheap grain, sugar, cotton, etc has a devastating effect when dumped on fragile Third World markets. US import duties are even more questionable: a shirt made by a Bangladeshi worker, for instance, attracts 20 times the import tax of one made in the EU.

HOT DOG HEAVEN

The great American hot dog is said to have been invented by street vendors in New York City, who sold them from barrows in the 1860s. The name was probably coined in around 1906 by cartoonist TA Dorgan, when he drew a dachshund sandwiched between an elongated bun. By this time George J French had launched the perfect accompaniment – French's mustard – and by 1939 the 'dog' was such a definitive part of US cuisine that President Franklin Roosevelt served one to the UK's King George VI. The love affair with the hot dog shows no sign of ending: each year, Americans eat an estimated 16 billion of them.

THE REAL THING

- John Pemberton, the inventor of Coca-Cola, referred to it as 'Esteemed Brain Tonic and Intellectual Beverage'.

- In 1919, the Candler family sold the Coca-Cola company to Ernest Wooduff for $25 million ($15 million). The company launched its curvy bottle in 1916. It was apparently designed to resemble a cola nut, and in 1945 'Coke' was registered as a trademark.

- Many of the details we associate with Santa Claus, including his fur trimmed red suit, were invented for a Coca-Cola advertising campaign in around 1890.

- Coca-Cola was first bottled in 1899 at a plant on Patten Parkway in downtown Chattanooga, Tennessee, after two local attorneys purchased the bottling rights to the popular soft drink for $1 (60p). Bargain!

WORK EXPERIENCE

Stars who employed Jimi Hendrix as a backing guitarist before he shot to fame with his band Work Experience:

- Little Richard
- The Isley Brothers
- Wilson Pickett
- BB King
- Sam Cooke
- Solomon Burke
- Chuck Jackson
- Jackie Wilson
- Ike and Tina Turner
- Curtis Knight

THANKSGIVING SPECIAL

- apricot brandy
- dry gin
- French vermouth
- 2 dashes lemon juice

Shake over ice, strain into a cocktail glass and top with a cherry.

DON'T MENTION THE GERMANS

The hamburger, America's greatest contribution to world cuisine, was supposedly invented in 1904 by Louis Lassen for customers at his 14-stool diner in New Haven, Connecticut. Big business got in on the act when White Castle, now the country's oldest hamburger chain, began dishing up steam-fried patties (18 per lb/20 per 500g of beef) and chopped onions for a nickel (3p) a time. Despite its success the burger suffered an identity crisis during World War II, when vendors thought its name smacked of enemy language and briefly rebranded it the 'Liberty Sandwich'. Since then, sales have climbed steadily, with around 8.2 billion sold in US commercial restaurants in 2001. McDonald's alone boasts 25,000 outlets in 115 different countries.

A PRESIDENTIAL MENAGERIE

The people of the United States have been led by: 6 oxen, 6 dogs, 5 pigs, 4 goats, 4 rats, 4 tigers, 3 monkeys, 3 dragons, 2 snakes, 2 roosters, 2 horses and 1 rabbit. That's according to Chinese horoscopes, of course.

Ox: William Harrison, Abraham Lincoln, Benjamin Harrison, William Taft, Richard Nixon, Gerald Ford

Dog: James Monroe, Martin Van Buren, Dwight Eisenhower, George Bush, Bill Clinton, George W Bush

Pig: John Adams, James Knox Polk, James Garfield, William McKinley, Ronald Reagan

Goat: Thomas Jefferson, John Quincy Adams, Andrew Jackson, James Buchanan

Rat: Zachary Taylor, Andrew Johnson, Woodrow Wilson, Jimmy Carter

Tiger: Ulysses Grant, Rutherford Hayes, Theodore Roosevelt, Franklin Roosevelt

Monkey: George Washington, Franklin Pierce, Lyndon Johnson

Dragon: Millard Fillmore, Calvin Coolidge, Harry Truman

Snake: Grover Cleveland, John F Kennedy

Rooster: Chester Arthur, Warren Harding

Horse: John Tyler, Herbert Hoover

Rabbit: James Madison

CHINESE HOROSCOPE CHARACTERISTICS

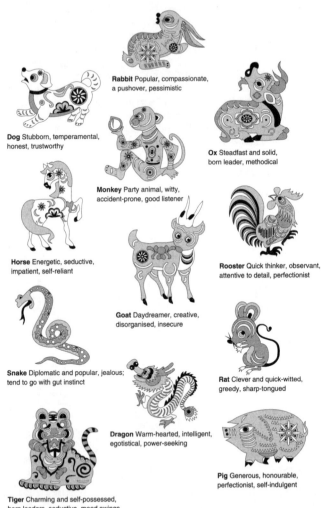

Rabbit Popular, compassionate, a pushover, pessimistic

Dog Stubborn, temperamental, honest, trustworthy

Ox Steadfast and solid, born leader, methodical

Monkey Party animal, witty, accident-prone, good listener

Horse Energetic, seductive, impatient, self-reliant

Rooster Quick thinker, observant, attentive to detail, perfectionist

Goat Daydreamer, creative, disorganised, insecure

Snake Diplomatic and popular, jealous; tend to go with gut instinct

Rat Clever and quick-witted, greedy, sharp-tongued

Dragon Warm-hearted, intelligent, egotistical, power-seeking

Pig Generous, honourable, perfectionist, self-indulgent

Tiger Charming and self-possessed, born leaders, seductive, mood swings

WATCHERS CHARTER

Travellers flying to and within the US now leave something behind after every trip – a slice of their personal life. Since the events of 9/11, new security laws require airlines to make booking details available to customs and immigration officers on demand. This is done electronically via a passenger name record (PNR), which, for example, can include your name, date of birth, date and time of flights, flight numbers, destination, stopovers, credit card and frequent-flier details, state of health, the kind of food you eat (sometimes useful for establishing a traveller's religion), who you travelled with, where and how long you stayed, and whether you required one bed or two! New information is added every time you fly, creating a detailed profile over several years. This flies in the face of EU data protection law, which says that personal data collected for one purpose (ie travelling) can't be used for another (ie government snooping) – however good the reason – without the subject's permission. This hasn't much worried the Americans, who don't allow non-compliant airlines to land.

'I DON'T THINK WE'RE IN KANSAS ANY MORE, TOTO'

- 'Tornado Alley' stretches across the states of Texas, Oklahoma, Arkansas, Kansas, Missouri, South Dakota, Tennessee, Iowa, Illinois and Indiana.

- Around 1,000 tornadoes occur every year, killing on average 80 people and leaving a trail of destruction behind them.

- The condition that creates such powerful natural phenomena is the meeting of the hot and humid air from the Gulf of Mexico and the drier, fresh air from California and Canada.

- April to June is the main tornado season.

- The strongest tornadoes can produce twisters with wind speeds up to 400kph (244mph). They can travel at more than 100 kph (62mph), and stay on the ground from 20 minutes to several hours.

- The worst tornado death toll ever recorded in the US was from the so-called 'Three States' tornado of 1925, which moved from Louisiana through Missouri, Illinois and Indiana, killing 689 people and making 11,000 homeless.

COSTLY CALL

When the first transatlantic phone call was made in 1927, it cost $75 (£45) for three minutes – half the cost of a car.

THE LAW 1, NORIEGA 0

One of the more successful law enforcement capers in American history was Operation Just Cause, launched on Wednesday 20 December 1989 to capture and charge Panamanian president Manuel Noriega. At the time, Noriega was described (by Senator Jesse Helms) as 'the biggest head of the biggest drug-trafficking operation in the western hemisphere'. More than 24,000 airborne US troops invaded Panama to discover that Manuel had a business appointment at a Tocumen brothel, 15km (10 miles) outside Panama City. He was eventually run to ground at the Papal ambassador's office, where he demanded sanctuary from the Catholic Church. The building was surrounded by Special Forces, who spent much of Christmas bombarding the place with ear-splitting pop music. According to Army folklore, Noriega finally cracked on 3 January 1990 after hearing The Clash's version of Sonny Curtis's classic 'I Fought The Law (And The Law Won)'.

SAN QUENTIN, YOU'VE BEEN THIRSTY WORK FOR ME

In 1969, when Johnny Cash played the notorious San Quentin prison, Marin County, California, for a live album and TV documentary, he was understandably nervous about the reaction of the prison guards. This was because his specially composed 'San Quentin' included lines such as 'San Quentin, I hate every inch of you' and 'San Quentin, you've been livin' hell to me'. As he finished the song, a bashful Cash asked: 'If any of the guards are still speaking to me, could I have a glass of water?' Despite persistent rumours in the 1960s that he was a hardened criminal who had done time, the truth is that Cash spent only a few days behind bars. He was twice locked up for possession of amphetamines, but the inspiration for his song 'Starkville City Jail' stemmed from a bizarre conviction for picking flowers in Mississippi.

SOME MILESTONES IN COMPUTER DEVELOPMENT

1930 The 'differential analyzer' (or analogue computer) is invented by Vannevar Bush at MIT in Boston.

1956 The first high-level programming language, FORTRAN, is invented by IBM (John Bachus).

1969 ARPANET, the precursor to the Internet, is started by the US Department of Defense.

1970 IBM introduce the floppy disc.

1971 Intel launch the microprocessor.

1975 IBM launch the laser printer.

1976 Steve Jobs and Stephen Wozniak start Apple computers.

1977 Apple II becomes the first mass-produced home computer.

1981 IBM launch their PC.

1984 Apple launch the Macintosh.

1989 Tim Berners-Lee develops the World Wide Web.

GROUNDHOG DAY

Traditionally, on this day in midwinter (2 February) the groundhog wakes from a long winter's nap, and goes outside of its den to see if it can see its shadow. According to legend, if the groundhog sees its shadow there will be six more weeks of winter. It then returns to its den and goes back to sleep. If it does not see its shadow, spring is just around the corner. The Groundhog Day tradition has German roots. As German immigrants settled in the hills of Pennsylvania, they began the tradition of using the groundhog to predict the arrival of spring. The tale seems to be based upon Candlemas – indeed, a famous Candlemas poem says:

If Candlemas be fair and bright,
Winter has another flight.
If Candlemas brings clouds and rain,
Winter will not come again.

Punxsutawney, Pennsylvania is the site of the annual groundhog event. The groundhog is called Punxsutawney Phil, and apparently sees his shadow about 9 out of 10 times.

MEMORIAL DAY

Friendship Cemetery in Columbus, Mississippi, has been called the place 'where flowers healed a nation'. It was 25 April 1866, and the Civil War had been over for a year when the ladies of Columbus decided to decorate both Confederate and Union soldiers' graves with beautiful bouquets and garlands of flowers. As a direct result of this thoughtful gesture, Americans celebrate what has come to be called Memorial Day each year, an annual observance or recognition of war dead.

SMALL IS BEAUTIFUL

Number of inhabitants **0**

Gulf City, Florida
Picket Lake, Minnesota
Sunday Lake, Minnesota
Promontory Point, Utah

 1

Ervings, New Hampshire
New Amsterdam, Indiana
Hibberts, Maine
Lost Springs, Wyoming

 2

Twombly, Maine
Success Township, New Hampshire
Hove Mobile Park, North Dakota
Oil Springs Reservation, Cattaraugus County, New York
Monowi, Nebraska

 3

North Red River Township, Minnesota
Rulien Township, Minnesota
Hush Lake, Minnesota
Pfeiffer Lake, Minnesota
Livermore, New Hampshire
Hillsview, South Dakota
Point of Rocks, Wyoming
Hobart Bay, Alaska
East Blythe, California

 4

Blacksville, Georgia
Northwest Hancock, Maine
Township 157–30, Minnesota
Beans, New Hampshire
Flat, Alaska

 5

Storrie, California
Bear Head Lake, Minnesota
Baker, Missouri
Gross, Nebraska
Odell Township, New Hampshire
Maza, North Dakota
Prudhoe Bay, Alaska
Somerset, Vermont

 6

Verdon, South Dakota
Kiel Township, Minnesota
Islandia, Florida
Tenney, Minnesota
Freeport, Kansas
Ruso, North Dakota
Cottonwood, South Dakota
Rawson, North Dakota
Marineland, Florida

 7

Forest Area Township, Minnesota
Cave, Missouri

8

Averill, Vermont
Hangaard Township, Minnesota

 9

Oil Springs Reservation, Allegany County, New York
Kaskaskia, Illinois, (former state capital)
Kingsbury, Maine
Florida, Missouri

ST PATRICK'S DAY

St Patrick's Day was celebrated in New York City for the first time at the Crown and Thistle Tavern on 17 March 1756. The ten longest-running St Patrick's Day parades in the USA are:

- New York, 1762
- Philadelphia, 1780
- Savannah, 1813
- Carbondale, Pennsylvania, 1833
- Chicago, 1843
- New Haven, Connecticut, 1845
- San Francisco, 1852
- Scranton, Pennsylvania, 1853
- Atlanta, 1858
- Cleveland, Ohio, 1867

The Chicago River is dyed green on St Patrick's Day.

10 'BIG APPLE' COCKTAILS

Name	Main ingredient	Other ingredients
Big Apple	Scotch, apple	Amaretto di Saronno, Drambuie, grenadine, lemon, ice, slice of apple
Bronx	dry gin	dry vermouth, sweet vermouth, orange juice, egg white, ice
Bronx Terrace	dry gin	dry vermouth, lime juice cordial, ice, a cherry
Brooklyn	rye whiskey	sweet vermouth, Amer Picón, maraschino, ice
Harlem	dry gin	pineapple juice, maraschino, ice, pineapple chunks
Long Island Tea	light rum	vodka, gin, cold tea, ice, cola, slice of lemon, sprig of mint
Manhattan Cooler	claret	dark rum, lemon juice, sugar, ice
Manhattan Skyscraper	bourbon whiskey	dry vermouth, angostura, dry ginger ale
New York Cooler	Canadian Club whiskey	lemon juice, grenadine, ice, soda water, slice of lemon
New York Sour	bourbon whiskey	lemon juice, sugar, ice, claret, cherry, slice of lemon

PUMPKIN TRIVIA

In 1584, after the French explorer Jacques Cartier explored the St Lawrence region of North America, he reported finding *gros melons* (large melons). The name was translated to English as 'pompions', which has since evolved into the modern 'pumpkin'. Weighing a whopping 509kg (1,140lb), the largest pumpkin was grown in 2000 by Dave Stelts of Leetonia, Ohio. The largest pumpkin pie ever made was 156kg (350lb) and 152cm (5ft) in diameter.

WINNING COMBINATION

The Three Caballeros by Walt Disney (1944) was the first film to combine live action and animation.

TITANIC PROFILE

Length	269m (882ft 9in)
Height *(measured from keel to funnel top)*	53.3m (175ft)
Width	28.2m (92ft 6in)
Gross tonnage	42,030 tonnes (46,329 tons)
Decks	10
Top speed	24 knots
Number of rivets	3 million
Number of anchors	2
Funnels	4, measuring 18.3m (60ft) high and 6.7m (22ft) wide
Passengers	2,435
Crew	885
Lifeboat capacity	1,178
Construction cost	$7.5 million (£4.5 million)

THE EMPIRE STATE BUILDING

The Empire State Building, a skyline symbol of New York, was built in 410 days at a cost of $41 million (£25 million). After opening in 1931, it remained the world's tallest building for 46 years. It stands 381m (1,250ft) to the 102nd-floor observatory. There are 1,860 steps from street level to the 102nd floor and 73 elevators, operating at speeds of 183–427m (600–1,400ft) a minute. The total length of the elevator shafts is 11km (7 miles), and there are 757km (473 miles) of electrical wire, which can deliver 40 million kilowatt-hours used by the building each year. Water to tanks at various levels is provided by 110km (70 miles) of piping, with the uppermost tank at the 101st floor. There is 5.2 million m (17 million ft) of telephone wire and the building has 6,500 vertical sliding windows. The total weight of the building is 330,000 tonnes (365,000 tons) and it has a volume of nearly 10.5 million cubic m (37 million cubic ft). It contains 10 million bricks, and more than 117 million people have visited the building. Its cost was considerably less than the expected $50 million (£30 million), due to the effect of the Great Depression. The cornerstone was laid by Alfred E Smith, former governor of New York, on 17 September 1930. The official opening – following seven million man-hours of labour – took place on 1 May 1931, when President Herbert Hoover symbolically pressed a button in Washington, DC to turn on the building's lights.

CHRISTMAS CARDS

German lithographer Louis Prang produced the first greetings card in the US. He had a workshop in Boston, Massachusetts, and started producing the first colour cards with winter scenes for Christmas and New Year.

It was during the American Civil War (at Abraham Lincoln's request) that political cartoonist Thomas Nast produced an illustration of Santa Claus to boost the spirits of the Union troops. He was the first to illustrate the red suit and big leather belt. Every year, Nast added more details to his representations, including the North Pole home and the Naughty and Nice list.

The most famous image of Santa Claus – and the one most people are familiar with today – was created by Haddon Sundblom in 1931 for a Coca-Cola commercial.

4 JULY – INDEPENDENCE DAY

'But what was most remarkable, Broadway being three miles long, and the booths lining each side of it, in every booth there was a roast pig, large or small, as the center attraction. Six miles of roast pig! And that in New York City alone; and roast pig in every other city, town, hamlet and village in the Union. What association can there be between roast pig and independence?'
Frederick Marryat, describing a Fourth of July celebration (1837)

The Declaration of Independence was not signed by all representatives until August 1776. To make it official, the last signatory – John Hancock, President of the Continental Congress – put his moniker on it, and from this came the expression 'to put your John Hancock on it'. To celebrate Independence Day, many cottage owners on lakes will set out flares along the shore to create a 'Ring of Fire'.

HOUSE ABOUT THAT!

The following figures were quoted by *The Almanac* in 1999 about the house being built by 'Oracle' multi-multi-multimillionaire Larry Ellison.

Preliminary estimated cost – $40 million (£24 million)
Current estimated cost – $60 million (£36.1 million)
Pounds (kg) of Yuba River rocks – 6 million (2.7 million)
Pounds (kg) of Chinese granite – 4 million (1.8 million)
Number of boxes of Native American artefacts found on site – 5
Amount the Town Hall estimates it's paid in total project fees – $257,000 (£155,000)
Amount of dirt excavated for lake – 30,000 cubic yards (22,000 cubic m)
Weight of one oak tree moved across site – 145,000lb (66,000kg)
Number of wells on property – 7
Weight of rock that will be inside master bath shower – 60,000lb (27,000kg)
Estimated number of workers on site each day – 100
Time for crew to place all landscaping stones – 12 to 18 months

20 YEARS OF EMMY FUNNIES

The TV series *Frasier* won five consecutive Emmy awards as best comedy (1994–8).

Cheers has won the prestigious award four times (1983, 1984, 1989 and 1991).

The *Mary Tyler Moore Show* has taken the trophy on three consecutive occasions (1975–7), as has *Taxi* (1979–81).

Shows that have won twice are *All In The Family* (1973, 1978), *The Golden Girls* (1986, 1987) and *Murphy Brown* (1990, 1992).

One-time winners are *M*A*S*H* (1974), *Barney Miller* (1982), *The Cosby Show* (1985), *The Wonder Years* (1988), *Seinfeld* (1993), *Ally McBeal* (1999), *Will And Grace* (2000), *Sex And The City* (2001), *Friends* (2002) and *Everybody Loves Raymond* (2003).

WIND-RESISTANT

Jefferson National Expansion Memorial, Missouri, consists of the Gateway Arch, the Museum of Westward Expansion and St Louis's Old Courthouse. During a nationwide competition in 1947–8, architect Eero Saarinen's inspired design for a 192m (630ft) stainless-steel arch was chosen as a perfect monument to the spirit of the Western pioneers. Its construction began in 1963 and was completed on 28 October 1965. The Arch has foundations sunk 18.3m (60ft) into the ground and is built to withstand earthquakes and high winds. It sways up to 2.5cm (1 inch) in a 32kph (20mph) wind, and can accommodate a swaying movement of up to 46cm (18in).

AROUND THE WORLD IN AMERICA

Alexandria, Minnesota
Alexandria, New Hampshire
Athens, Georgia
Athens, Kentucky
Athens, Ohio
Bethlehem, Pennsylvania
Birmingham, Alabama
Bristol, Rhode Island
Cairo, Illinois
Cambridge, Massachusetts
Dover, Delaware
Dover, New Hampshire
Dresden, Ohio
Exeter, New Hampshire
Fife, Montana
Florence, Oregon
Greenwich, Connecticut
Londonderry, New Hampshire
Madrid, Iowa
Manchester, New Hampshire
Marathon, Florida
Milan, Kansas

Moscow, Idaho
Nazareth, Pennsylvania
New Amsterdam, Indiana
Newport, Rhode Island
Odessa, Delaware
Paris, Kentucky
Paris, Texas
Peru, Indiana
Portsmouth, Rhode Island
Prague, Nebraska
Rome, Georgia
Rome, Kansas
Rugby, North Dakota
St Petersburg, Florida
Somerset, Vermont
Stuttgart, Arkansas
Troy, New York
Venice, Florida
Versailles, Kentucky
Warsaw, Missouri
Waterloo, Indiana
Westminster, Colorado

BUILDING BILLS

American paper money has shown historic buildings from as early as 1860, when the United States Capitol Building was first illustrated (at the moment it appears on the back of the $50 note). Since 1929, monuments have appeared on the back of most US currency. The current $5 bill has a portrait of Abraham Lincoln on the front and a picture of the Lincoln Memorial on the reverse. The $10 bill has a picture of Alexander Hamilton (first secretary of the Treasury) on its front side and a view of the Treasury Building on the back. The $100 bill has Benjamin Franklin on the front and Independence Hall in Philadelphia (where he lived) on the back. The White House appeared on the back of the $20 note in 1929. The 1948 restoration of the White House, during which a balcony was added to the second floor, is featured on the current $20 bill.

INDEPENDENCE DAY PUNCH

- 1kg (2lb) sugar
- 500ml (1 pint) lemon juice
- 3 bottles claret
- 1 bottle cognac
- 1 bottle champagne

Stir, then add six sliced lemons and ice cubes.

HALLOWEEN

Total US pumpkin production in 2001 was a staggering 377 million kg (831.2 million lb). Illinois, with a production of 144 million kg (319 million lb), led the country. There also were big pumpkin patches in California (73 million kg/162 million lb produced), New York (61 million kg/134 million lb), Pennsylvania (45 million kg/99 million lb), Ohio (27 million kg/59 million lb) and Michigan (26 million kg/58 million lb). The total value of all these pumpkins was £42 million ($71 million).

FAMOUS VEGETARIANS

In the past
Louisa May Alcott – writer
Clara Barton – nurse and first president of the American Red Cross
Isadora Duncan – dancer
Benjamin Franklin – American statesman, philosopher and scientist
Jerry Garcia – musician

Present-day vegetarians

Alec Baldwin – actor
Kim Basinger – actor
Bob Dylan – musician
Danny DeVito – actor, director
David Duchovny – actor
Peter Falk – actor
Richard Gere – actor
Elliott Gould – actor
Daryl Hannah – actor
Dustin Hoffman – actor
Janet Jackson – singer
Michael Jackson – singer
Billie Jean King – tennis champion

Carl Lewis – Olympic athlete
Madonna – musician
Steve Martin – actor and comedian
Meatloaf – singer
Martina Navratilova – tennis champion
Olivia Newton-John – singer, actor
Claudia Schiffer – supermodel
Dave Scott – six-time Ironman triathlon winner
Tina Turner – singer
Lindsay Wagner – actor

HAUNTING HALLOWEEN LOCATIONS

- Transylvania County, North Carolina
- Tombstone, Arizona
- Pumpkin Center, North Carolina
- Pumpkin Bend township, Arkansas
- Cape Fear township (New Hanover County), North Carolina
- Cape Fear township (Chatham County), North Carolina
- Skull Creek township, Nebraska

'UNLUCKY' – DIED ON THE 13TH

13 January 1929 – Wyatt Earp, gunslinger
13 January 1978 – Hubert H Humphrey, vice president of the United States
13 March 1901 – Benjamin Harrison, 23rd president of the United States
13 May 1961 – Gary Cooper, actor
13 June 1986 – Benny Goodman, musician
13 October 1974 – Ed Sullivan, TV host
13 November 1974 – Karen Silkwood, union activist
13 December 1961 – Grandma Moses, artist

IDENTITY CRISIS

Within its 400-year history, six different flags have flown over Texas. First came
the colonial Spanish, while in some neighbourhoods the French were the
governing nation. After the Louisiana Purchase in 1803 – when France sold
its stake in the region to the Americans – Texas became tenuously neutral
until, in 1821, it was incorporated into the newly independent state of Mexico.
Texans rebelled against Mexican rule and for a spell were independent, proudly
hoisting their own flag, before joining the US. In the Civil War (1861–5),
Texas stood squarely behind the Confederates, adopting its famous ensign.
In 1870, Texas was – for the second time – readmitted to the Union.

ST PATRICK'S DAY COCKTAIL

- white crème de menthe
- Irish whiskey
- green Chartreuse
- angostura.

  Stir over ice, then strain into a cocktail glass

ON THIS DAY...

13 October 1792 The cornerstone of the White House was laid.

13 September 1862 Union soldiers find Robert E Lee's battle plans in a field outside Frederick, Maryland.

13 March 1925 A law was passed in Tennessee, prohibiting the teaching of the theory of evolution.

13 September 1999 During the 1970s science fiction TV series *Space: 1999*, this was the day the Moon broke away from its orbit around the Earth and began its voyage across the universe, taking the inhabitants of Moon Base Alpha with it.

13 February 2000 The last original *Peanuts* comic strip appeared in a newspaper the day after the death of its creator, Charles M Schultz.

13 February 2002 Queen Elizabeth II gave former New York City mayor Rudolph Giuliani an honorary knighthood.

13 July 2002 A lightning strike set off the Sour Biscuit Fire in Oregon and northern California, which had burned 202,200 hectares (499,570 acres) when it was finally contained, on 5 September.

THANKSGIVING

'Thanksgiving is America's national chow-down feast, the one occasion each year when gluttony becomes a patriotic duty. (In France, by contrast, there are three such days: Hier, Aujourd'Hui and Demain.)' *Michael Dresser*

'The king and high priest of all the festivals was the autumn Thanksgiving. When the apples were all gathered and the cider was all made, and the yellow pumpkins were rolled in from many a hill in billows of gold, and the corn was husked, and the labors of the season were done, and the warm, late days of Indian Summer came in, dreamy, and calm, and still, with just enough frost to crisp the ground of a morning, but with warm traces of benignant, sunny hours at noon, there came over the community a sort of genial repose of spirit – a sense of something accomplished.'
Harriet Beecher Stowe

THE FRISBEE...

...was invented in 1925 by Yale students, who began hurling empty plates that had previously been used by the Frisbie Baking Company to hold pies.

COMIC BOOK CHARACTERS

Character	Name	Physical statistics	First appearance
Spider-Man	Peter Parker	178cm (5ft 10in) 75kg (165lb)	1962: *Amazing Fantasy 15*
Superman	Clark Kent	191cm (6ft 3in) 102kg (225lb)	1938
Batman	Bruce Wayne	188cm (6ft 2in) 97kg (215lb)	1939: *Detective Comics*
Captain America	Steve Rogers	188cm (6ft 2in) 109kg (240lb)	1941: *Captain America Comics 1*
Captain Marvel	Mar-Vell (alias Dr Walter Lawson)	188cm (6ft 2in) 109kg (240lb)	*Marvel Superheroes 18*
Daredevil	Matthew Michael Murdock	183cm (6ft) 91kg (200lb)	*Daredevil 1 vol. 1*
Silver Surfer	Norrin Radd	194cm (6ft 4in) Weight unknown	*Fantastic Four vol. 148*

FAMILY TRAGEDY

Five brothers were among the dead when a Japanese submarine torpedoed the *USS Juneau* in the Battle of Guadalcanal on 13 November 1942. George, Francis, Joseph, Matt and Al Sullivan from Waterloo, Iowa, all enlisted in the aftermath of Pearl Harbour and insisted on serving together. They were among around 700 victims when the Japanese torpedo ploughed into the ship's ammunition hold. Fewer than a dozen of the crew survived.

After this tragic event, the US military made a policy decision to keep siblings on active service apart. Fifty years after the brothers' deaths a destroyer called *USS The Sullivans* was launched in Maine by Kelly Sullivan, granddaughter of the youngest brother, Al.

THE FIRST NORTH AMERICAN THANKSGIVING

This is believed to have been held in Virginia in 1619 or 1621. President Abraham Lincoln proclaimed Thanksgiving a national holiday in 1863. Since 1947, the National Turkey Federation (NTF) has presented the President of the United States with a live turkey and two dressed turkeys in celebration of the holiday. After the ceremony, the live bird retires to a historical farm to live out the rest of its years. It has been estimated that 95 per cent of Americans eat turkey at Thanksgiving. According to the National Turkey Federation, about 24 per cent of Americans purchase fresh turkeys for Thanksgiving, and 69 per cent purchase frozen ones.

10 SOUTHERN COCKTAILS

Name	Main Ingredient	Other Ingredients
Alabama Fizz	gin	lemon juice, sugar, ice, soda, mint
Florida Daiquiri	white rum	lime juice, maraschino, crushed ice, cherry
Georgia Mint Julep	brandy	peach brandy, sugar, mint, ice
Bittersweet	vermouth	orange bitters, orange twist
Kentucky Sunset	bourbon whiskey	anisette, strega, ice, twist of orange
Louisiana Lullaby	Jamaican rum	red Dubonnet, Grand Marnier, ice, slice of lemon
Mississippi Planters	brandy	white rum, bourbon whiskey, punch, lemon juice, sugar syrup, ice, soda water
New Orleans Buck	white rum	orange juice, lemon juice, ice, ginger ale
New Orleans Fizz	gin	lime juice, lemon juice, orange flower water, Gomme syrup, cream, ice, soda water
Savannah	dry gin	orange juice, egg white, crème de cacao, ice

AMERICAN GRAVESTONE EPITAPHS

'Life, not Death, is the Great Adventure'
Writer **Sherwood Anderson**
(Virginia)

'Excuse My Dust'
Writer **Dorothy Parker**

'And away we go!'
Comic **Jackie Gleason**

'Here lies
Lester Moore
Four slugs from a .44
No Les
No more'
(Tombstone, Nevada)

'I have not yet begun to fight'
John Paul Jones
(US Naval Academy, Maryland)

'I told you I was sick'
Anonymous
(Georgia)

'Here lies
Johnny Yeast
Pardon me
For not rising'
(New Mexico)

'Here lies old **Rastus Sominy**
Died a-eating hominy
In 1859 anno domini'
(Georgia)

'I was Carolina born
And Carolina bred
And here I lay
Carolina dead'
Anonymous
(North Carolina)

'She drank good ale
Good punch and wine
And lived to the age of 99'
Anonymous
(New Jersey)

'I was somebody'
Anonymous
(Vermont)

'Here lies an atheist
All dressed up
And no place to go'
Anonymous
(Maryland)

LIGHTNING STRIKES TWICE

To prove that lightning was a form of electricity, Benjamin Franklin famously flew a kite in a storm with a metal key tied to the kite string. Sparks came from the key after the lightning was attracted to the kite and, although Franklin survived his foolhardy experimentation, two other people were killed when they copied it. However, his insistence about the value of earthed, metal lightning conductors on tall buildings led to the installation of 400 conductors in Philadelphia alone by 1782.

LESSER KNOWN FACTS ABOUT GEORGE WASHINGTON

He had wooden false teeth. Replacement gnashers at the time were generally made of gold, bone or agate, or were even pulled from the jaws of the dead.

His foxhound dogs were called Drunkard, Tipler and Tipsy.

No one really knows what he looked like. Modern perceptions of his facial features are based on the 14 portraits by artist Charles Willson Peale. However, the painter was noted for making all his eminent subjects look rather alike.

Those waiting with bated breath for George Washington's second inaugural speech experienced something of an anticlimax. The speech amounted to a mere 135 words – the shortest inaugural speech in the history of the US. However, perhaps its brevity was a good omen, since William Henry Harrison (whose speech in 1841 lasted nearly two hours) stayed in office for a paltry 32 days.

THE KID'LL NEVER MAKE IT

In 1978, a lanky 15-year-old youth from Brooklyn, New York, got dropped from his high-school basketball team. Three years later, Virginia and UCLA universities didn't even respond to his applications to play for them. Oh dear... The youth concerned was one Michael Jordan, who by 1983 was not only wowing crowds but also reshaping the game's rules. Coaches at North Carolina had to show slow-motion video clips to referees to prove they were wrong to penalise him for travelling violations. The film showed that Jordan moved faster than the eye could see. With the Chicago Bulls, he went on to win six NBA (National Basketball Asscoiation) championships during the 1990s and was voted Most Valuable Player on five occasions. He holds the NBA record for most seasons as leading scorer (10).

NOTORIOUS

In 1993, Lorena Bobbitt used a kitchen knife to sever her husband John Wayne's penis as he slept. She then drove off, tossing the mutilated manhood in a field as she went, although the penis was recovered and reattached during a nine-hour operation. She was cleared of malicious wounding on the grounds of temporary insanity. He was later acquitted of raping her. Lorena went on to found the Lorena Bobbitt Foundation for domestic violence victims. Meanwhile, John starred in two porn movies and then became a priest in the Universal Life Church in Las Vegas.

ODOUR-RATED

When viewers stayed away from the cinema and turned onto television in the late 1950s, there were two attempts to regain audiences by bringing them the odour of action. Aroma-Rama competed with Smell-O-Vision as two new ways to lure people back to the silver screen. The first had scents filtered through existing air-conditioning systems, while the second had the necessary film smells piped to individual seats. As it happened, neither system was a winner, with only one film being made for each method. The notion was an old one: perfume had been sprayed in a cinema in Pennsylvania in 1906, and later it was used to improve the impact of talkies.

CREEPY CRAWLIES

Some American town names to give you the creepy crawlies:

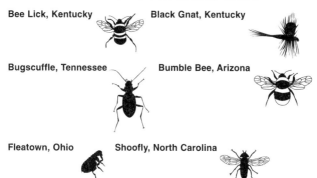

Bee Lick, Kentucky   **Black Gnat, Kentucky**

Bugscuffle, Tennessee   **Bumble Bee, Arizona**

Fleatown, Ohio   **Shoofly, North Carolina**

BAD DREAM

A plaque intended to mark the achievements of black actor James Earl Jones – the voice of Darth Vader in *Star Wars* – was erroneously made out in the name of James Earl Ray, convicted killer of black activist Martin Luther King. Drawn up on behalf of Lauderhill, Florida (the actor's home city) at the start of 2002, it was to have been presented to Jones as the guest speaker at the annual Martin Luther King celebration day, using phraseology reminiscent of the eloquent civil rights leader. Thanks to a blunder apparently made by a non-English-speaking employee at the sign factory, it read, 'Thank you, James Earl Ray, for Keeping the Dream Alive.'

BOB DYLAN'S WOMEN – AN A–Z OF GIRLS' NAMES IN HIS SONG TITLES

'Absolutely Sweet Marie'
'Angelina'
'Bessie Smith'
'Corrina, Corrina'
'Delia'
'Denise'
'Farewell Angelina'
'Gypsy Lou'
'Hazel'
'In Search Of Little Sadie'
'Katie's Been Gone'
'Lily Of The West'
'Lily, Rosemary And The Jack Of Hearts'
'Little Maggie'
'Little Sadie'
'Maggie's Farm'
'Mary Ann'
'Peggy Day'
'Pretty Peggy-O'
'Queen Jane Approximately'
'Rita May'
'Sally Sue Brown'
'Sara'
'Sarah Jane'
'Take A Message To Mary'
'The Lonesome Death Of Hattie Carroll'
'To Ramona'
'Visions Of Johanna'

VERTICALLY CHALLENGED AMERICANS

- Bonnie Parker – of Bonnie and Clyde – 147cm (4ft 10in)
- Estelle Getty – actress (*The Golden Girls*) – 150cm (4ft 11in)
- Margaret Mitchell – author – 152cm (5ft 0in)
- Dolly Parton – singer – 152cm (5ft 0in)
- Danny DeVito – actor – 152cm (5ft 0in)
- Paul Simon – singer – 157.5cm (5ft 2in)
- Prince – singer – 159cm (5ft 2½in)
- Sammy Davis Jr – entertainer – 160cm (5ft 3in)
- James Madison – shortest US president – 162.5cm (5ft 4in)
- Mel Brooks – director –162.5cm (5ft 4in)
- Michael J Fox – actor – 162.5cm (5ft 4in)
- George 'Baby Face' Nelson – gangster – 164cm (5ft 4¾in)
- Charles Manson – criminal – 165cm (5ft 5in)
- Harry Houdini – escapologist – 165cm (5ft 5in)

FOOD FOR THOUGHT

'Americans can eat garbage, provided you sprinkle it liberally with ketchup, mustard, chili sauce, Tabasco sauce, cayenne pepper or any other condiment which destroys the original flavor of the dish.' *Henry Miller*

'You can tell a lot about a fellow's character by his way of eating jellybeans.' *Ronald Reagan*

The *New York Times* has described the bagel as 'an unsweetened doughnut with rigor mortis'.

'When we lose, I eat. When we win, I eat. I also eat when we're rained out.' *Tommy Lasorda* (Dodgers baseball team manager)

'They say that you may always know the grave of a Virginian as, from the quantity of julep he has drunk, mint invariably springs up where he has been buried.' *Frederick Marryat* (1839)

'New Orleans food is as delicious as the less criminal forms of sin.' *Mark Twain* (1884)

'An average of two rodent hairs per one hundred grams of peanut butter is allowed.' *Food and Drug Administration* – government guidelines

LAST MEALS

According to *The Great Food Almanac* by Irena Chalmers, the last food that passed Elvis Presley's lips was four scoops of ice cream and six chocolate chip cookies.

Between December 1982 and July 2003, 307 Death Row inmates in Texas were required to place requests for their last meal:

- 53 declined to order a last meal
- 1 requested that a meal should be given to a homeless person
- 1 requested the Eucharist sacrament
- 1 requested 'Justice, equality, world peace'
- 1 requested 'Justice, temperance with mercy'
- 1 requested 'God's saving grace, love, truth, peace and freedom'

Possibly the largest meal was ordered by Stanley Baker Jr: two 450g (16oz) rib-eye steaks, 450g (16oz) turkey breast (sliced thin), 12 strips of bacon, two large hamburgers with mayo, onion and lettuce, two large baked potatoes with butter, sour cream, cheese and chives, four slices of cheese or 225g (8oz) grated cheddar cheese, chef salad with blue cheese dressing, two ears of corn on the cob, one pint of mint chocolate chip ice cream and four vanilla Cokes or Mr Pibb.

It should be noted at this point that the Texas Department of Criminal Justice makes the point that 'The final meal requested may not reflect the actual final meal served.'

AMERICA'S CUP

The equivalent of the Indy 500 on water, this is considered the Holy Grail of the maritime racing world. While there is no prize, apart from the coveted cup, teams from across the world will go to extraordinary – and extremely costly – lengths to wrest it from each other. The first race took place on 22 August 1851 around the Isle of Wight, England, the winning craft being a US schooner by the name of *America*.

AMERICANISMS

Ahtellyawhut – a way to start a sentence in Texas

Alien – non-American or small, green man with one eye and two antennae

All righty – affirmative response first spoken in Minnesota and popularised by Jim Carrey in the *Pet Detective* series

Bodega – corner shop

Grinder – meat sandwich also known as a 'hoagie', 'submarine', 'po'boy' or 'Cuban'

Hokey dokey – Minnesotan version of 'yes'

Hookup – either a mains connection for a camper van or a one-night stand – use with care

Howdy – the way in which tourists greet Americans

Jump the shark – the point at which the storylines in a long-running TV show become noticeably weak; taken from an episode of *Happy Days* when the Fonz went surfing and jumped over a shark

K-Mart Express – a cheap and easy date, inspired by 'K-Mart' (purveyor of cheap goods in the US) and 'express' (as in 'swift')

Mouse potato – Internet generation's take on the couch potato

Netizen – someone who spends too much time on the Internet

Riding the dog – a passage on a Greyhound bus – use with extreme care

Scalawags – southern whites with northern sympathies

Schlock – tat

Shucks – shucks

Stick – manual gears

Uff da – All-purpose phrase brought out of Scandinavia and into America to illustrate bumper stickers

Y'all – everyone in present company

Yessir – affirmative response

NATIVE AMERICAN SYMBLOLS

Totem poles were emblems used by Native Americans that symbolised where a person stood within a big family grouping — not just a mother, father, sister, brother, but within a whole clan of relatives.

In a Native kinship system, people were considered related:
• by blood;
• by experience;
• by war exploits;
• by adoption.

Each clan identified very strongly with the crests and figures carved on their totem pole.

CHEVY CHASE

US coastguards found themselves in a Chevy chase when innovative would-be immigrants converted a 1951 Chevrolet lorry to an ocean-going vessel in order to breach America's border controls. The lorry, kept afloat by empty 210 litre (55 gallon) oil drums strapped to its sides, got to within 65km (40 miles) of America before it was intercepted by the Coast Guard in July 2003. The chase was soon over, however, as the lorry powered by a propeller attached to the drive shaft, travelled at just 13kph (8mph). Its eight occupants were sent back to Cuba, from where they had originated.

CIVIL RIGHTS TIMELINE

1954: The US Supreme Court rules on a landmark case that unanimously agrees that segregation in schools is unconstitutional. The Supreme Court's ruling paves the way for a major desegregation programme in schools.

1955: In Montgomery, Alabama, civil rights worker Rosa Lee Parks refuses to give up her seat at the front of a bus to a white passenger, in defiance of a southern custom of the time. Her subsequent arrest sparked a bus boycott which lasted for more than a year, whereupon buses were desegregated.

1957: Establishment of the SCLC (Southern Christian Leadership Conference) by Reverend Martin Luther King Jr, Fred Shuttleworth and Charles K Steele. King is made president of the SCLC, a pivotal force in the civil rights movement.

An all-white school in Little Rock, Arkansas, finds the passage to segregation more problematic than first thought. Black students seeking to enter the school are blocked by crowds and President Eisenhower is forced to intervene with federal troops and the National Guard.

1960: The Greensboro Four make headlines when they begin a sit-in at a segregated Woolworth's lunch counter. The four black students were refused service but were not removed from the premises. Their action sparked many other non-violent protests throughout the South.

The formation of the SNCC (Student Non-Violent Coordinating Committee) provides young blacks with an organised framework for civil rights movement. The leadership of Stokely Carmichael sees the organisation become ever more radical.

1961: Student volunteers of CORE (Congress Of Racial Equality) send volunteer students out on bus trips to establish the effectiveness of new laws prohibiting segregation on interstate travel. The students become known as 'freedom riders'. A bus in Alabama that the freedom riders are on is set on fire, but they remain undeterred, and hundreds of black and white volunteers continue to volunteer as 'freedom riders'.

1963: Civil Rights leader Medgar Evers is murdered outside his home. White supremacist Byron De La Beckwith is acquitted twice in 1964. He is convicted of Evers' death 30 years later.

Nearly a quarter of a million people attend the March on Washington on 28 August. Massing at the Lincoln Memorial, the crowds listen to Martin Luther King Jr deliver his famous 'I Have A Dream' speech.

A Sunday school in Birmingham, Alabama, witnesses a tragedy as four young girls are killed by a bomb. The location of the bomb was at a well-known civil rights meeting point. In the aftermath of the tragedy, rioting erupts in Birmingham, with two further black youths losing their lives.

1964: A combination of civil rights groups that include CORE and SNCC spearheads a campaign to register black voters during a period that becomes known as Freedom Summer. Delegates are also sent to the Democratic National Convention in an attempt to disrupt and unseat the all-white Mississippi contingent.

President Johnson makes history on 2 July with the signing of the Civil Rights Act (1964). The Act prohibited segregation in public places and outlawed discrimination in employment.

Three young black Americans – Andrew Goodman, James E Cheney and Michael Schwerner – disappear after being released from police custody in Mississippi. All three are civil rights workers and had been arrested on speeding charges. They are released by police into the custody of the Ku Klux Klan. Their bodies are discovered after President Johnson mobilises the military to look for them.

1965: Malcolm X is assassinated in Harlem. The founder of the Organization of Afro-American Unity is believed to have been killed by black Muslims.

A march to Montgomery, Alabama, to support voting rights for blacks is stopped by a police blockade at Pettus Bridge. Many are injured by the police tactics of resorting to tear gas, beatings and whippings.

The Voting Rights Act (1965) passes through Congress, paving the way for easier registration to vote for southern blacks.

1968: Martin Luther King Jr is assassinated on a hotel balcony. Escaped convict James Earl Ray claims to have shot him. He recants this, however, after being convicted, speaking of a government conspiracy. Ray dies in jail having never had enough evidence to support his conspiracy theory. The circumstances surrounding King's death remain murky to this day.

The Civil Rights Act (1968) is signed by President Johnson, prohibiting discrimination in rental, sale and finance of housing.

1988: Congress overrules President Reagan and passes the Civil Rights Restoration Act (1988).

LIFE STORY

When the American magazine *Life* launched in 1936, its first cover featured a newborn baby, George Story, with the strapline 'Life begins'. Having won a reputation as the '*Life* baby', Story continued to feature in the magazine and readers were told about his two marriages, his becoming a dad and his retirement. Story's face also appeared in the final issue of the magazine in May 2000, with the headline 'A life ends'. Curiously, he died from heart failure just a few days later, his life story mirroring that of the magazine almost exactly.

WHAT'S IT WORTH?

$	US Dollar	1.0
£	GB pound	0.597642
£	Canadian pound	1.31808
€	Euro	0.858940
$	Australian dollar	1.44218

As on 13 October 2003

WORDS THE DYLAN WAY

He may or may not be the world's greatest living poet, but Bob Dylan isn't a great one for academic analysis of the cadence, rhythm, paraphrasing and pronoun use that drive enthusiasts into raptures. Asked how he was inspired to write 'Lay, Lady, Lay', the nasal crooner replied: 'The song came out of those first four chords. I filled it up with lyrics then, the la la la type thing.' So now we know.

On the subject of chords, that other great US folk hero, Johnny Cash, had some pertinent comments for every show-off electric guitarist (ie all of them). 'It doesn't matter to me that I only know three or four chords,' Cash wrote on the cover of his 1994 album *American Recordings*. 'All that matters is that the guitar and I are one.'

NATIONAL GROUPS IN THE US

NAACP	National Association for the Advancement of Colored People
NARA	National Archives and Records Administration
NASA	National Aeronautics and Space Administration
NBA	National Basketball Association
NCAA	National Collegiate Athletic Association
NFL	National Football League
NHL	National Hockey League
NIH	National Institutes of Health
NIST	National Institute of Standards and Technology
NOAA	National Oceanic and Atmospheric Administration
NOW	National Organization for Women
NPR	National Public Radio
NPS	National Park Service
NRA	National Recreation Area
NRA	National Rifle Association
NSF	National Science Foundation
NWR	National Wildlife Refuge

A NOSE FOR SUCCESS

When, following an operation, boxer Melvin Burkhart discovered that he could insert a 13cm (5in) nail into his nose, he hung up his gloves and joined the circus as a sideshow freak. During a 60-year career as 'the human blockhead', he drove ice picks and other assorted implements into his nasal passages and further developed skills as a sword swallower, snake wrestler and fire-eater. He could also suck his stomach in as far as his spine and inflate his lungs one at a time. Burkhart – from Louisville, Kentucky – worked with other human wonders, including the Seal Boy, the Amazing Petrified Man, the Two-Faced Man and his wife, Mildred the Alligator Girl. When freak shows went out of style, he became a children's entertainer. Burkhart died in Florida in 2001, at the age of 94.

RUSSIAN DEAD

There are three (well, technically 2½) Americans buried at the Kremlin in Russia: John Silas Reed, Charles Ruthenberg and half of the ashes of Bill Haywood. (The other half are in Chicago.)

COMETH THE HOUR

Continental America's four time zones were imposed in 1883 by US railroad companies frustrated at having to draw up timetables for trains travelling to numerous destinations, each with their own take on the time. When it is 9am in the Pacific Time Zone, it is 10am in the neighbouring Mountain Time Zone. Then comes the Central Time Zone, at 11am, and finally the Eastern Time Zone, at noon. The time zones work out their clocks in relation to Greenwich, London. There are two other time zones to consider, though: Alaska Time Zone, four hours behind the Eastern Time Zone; and the Hawaii-Aleutian Time Zone, one hour later than Alaska.

VICE PRESIDENTS OF THE UNITED STATES

Vice president	Party	Term	President
John Adams	Federalist	1789–97	Washington
Thomas Jefferson	Democratic-Republican	1797–1801	J Adams
Aaron Burr	Democratic-Republican	1801–5	Jefferson
George Clinton	Democratic-Republican	1805–9	Jefferson
George Clinton[1]	Democratic-Republican	1809–12	Madison
Elbridge Gerry[1]	Democratic-Republican	1813–14	Madison
Daniel D Tompkins	Democratic-Republican	1817–25	Monroe
John C Calhoun	Democratic-Republican	1825–9	JQ Adams
John C Calhoun[2]	Democratic-Republican	1829–32	Jackson
Martin Van Buren	Democratic	1833–7	Jackson
Richard M Johnson	Democratic	1837–41	Van Buren
John Tyler[3]	Whig	1841	WH Harrison
George M Dallas	Democratic	1845–9	Polk
Millard Fillmore[3]	Whig	1849–50	Taylor
William RD King[1]	Democratic	1853	Pierce
John C Breckinridge	Democratic	1857–61	Buchanan
Hannibal Hamlin	Republican	1861–5	Lincoln
Andrew Johnson[3]	Democratic	1865	Lincoln
Schuyler Colfax	Republican	1869–73	Grant
Henry Wilson[1]	Republican	1873–5	Grant
William A Wheeler	Republican	1877–81	Hayes
Chester A Arthur[3]	Republican	1881	Garfield
Thomas A Hendricks[1]	Democratic	1885	Cleveland
Levi P Morton	Republican	1889–93	B Harrison
Adlai E Stevenson	Democratic	1893–7	Cleveland
Garret A Hobart[1]	Republican	1897–9	McKinley

Theodore Roosevelt[3]	Republican	1901	McKinley
Charles W Fairbanks	Republican	1905–9	T Roosevelt
James S Sherman[1]	Republican	1909–12	Taft
Thomas R Marshall	Democratic	1913–21	Wilson
Calvin Coolidge[3]	Republican	1921–3	Harding
Charles G Dawes	Republican	1925–9	Coolidge
Charles Curtis	Republican	1929–33	Hoover
John N Garner	Democratic	1933–41	FD Roosevelt
Henry A Wallace	Democratic	1941–5	FD Roosevelt
Harry S Truman[3]	Democratic	1945	FD Roosevelt
Alben W Barkley	Democratic	1949–53	Truman
Richard M Nixon	Republican	1953–61	Eisenhower
Lyndon B Johnson[3]	Democratic	1961–3	Kennedy
Hubert H Humphrey	Democratic	1965–9	LB Johnson
Spiro T Agnew[2]	Republican	1969–73	Nixon
Gerald R Ford[4]	Republican	1973–4	Nixon
Nelson Rockefeller	Republican	1974–7	Ford
Walter Mondale	Democratic	1977–81	Carter
George HW Bush	Republican	1981–9	Reagan
J Danforth Quayle	Republican	1989–93	GHW Bush
Albert Gore	Democratic	1993–2001	Clinton
Richard B Cheney	Republican	2001–	GW Bush

Notes

1 Died in office.

2 Resigned as vice president.

3 Succeeded to presidency on death of president.

4 Succeeded to the presidency upon the resignation of the president.

Source: Dan Quayle Center, home of the United States Vice Presidential Museum,
Huntington, Indiana

VINE MAN

On 9 July 1922, at the age of 18, Johnny Weissmuller became the first man
to swim 100m in less than a minute. Within five years, he held every freestyle
swimming record from 100 yards (91.4m) to half a mile (800m). Famous for
his physique, he was approached by MGM to play the role of Tarzan and
subsequently played the 'King of the Jungle' in 13 films before being shuffled
off the silver screen when the series lost its public appeal. Before retirement,
he later returned as 'Jungle Jim' for a further dozen big screen outings –
once again in combat with the terrors of the equatorial forest.

TRIPLE CROWN WINNERS OF THE KENTUCKY DERBY

Year	Winner	Time	Jockey
1882	Apollo (Gelding)	2:40	Babe Hurd
1888	Macbeth II (Gelding)	2:38	George Covington
1914	Old Rosebud (Gelding)	2:03	John McCabe
1919	Sir Barton	2:09	Johnny Loftus
1930	Gallant Fox	2:07	Earl Sande
1935	Omaha	2:05	Willie Saunders
1937	War Admiral	2:03	Charley Kurtsinger
1941	Whirlaway	2:01	Eddie Arcaro
1943	Count Fleet	2:04	Johnny Longden
1946	Assault	2:06	Warren Mehrtens
1948	Citation	2:05	Eddie Arcaro
1973	Secretariat	1:59	Ron Turcotte
1977	Seattle Slew	2:02	Jean Cruguet
1978	Affirmed	2:01	Steve Cauthen

Note: From 1875 to 1895, the distance of the Kentucky Derby was 1 1/2 miles (2.4km). Since 1895, the Kentucky Derby distance has been 1 1/4 miles (2km).

IMMIGRANTS WHO MADE IT BIG IN AMERICA

Harry Houdini Born Ehrich Weisz in Hungary, he moved to America in 1878, at the age of 4, with his father (a rabbi) and the rest of his family. Houdini went on to become the greatest escapologist of the age.

Rudolph Valentino Born Rodolpho Guglielmi in southern Italy, in December 1913 Valentino set sail for the States (aged 18), in a suit lined with newspaper to keep out the cold. Soon he was a trailblazing Hollywood heartthrob.

Errol Flynn Son of a professor, Errol Flynn (Leslie Thomson) was born and brought up in Hobart, Tasmania. He later spent time in Australia and England, usually one step ahead of the law, until a role in a film at Elstree Studios brought him to the attention of a talent scout. He subsequently took Hollywood by storm, although publicists fabricated a childhood in Ireland for him, to mask the less than savoury nature of his early years.

Bob Hope Bob Hope (Leslie Townes) was born in London in 1903. The comedian emigrated to the USA with his parents in 1907. After some years on stage as a dancer and comedian, he made his first appearance on screen in 1938.

Cary Grant Born into poverty in Bristol, England, Cary Grant (Archibald Leach) joined a team of acrobats at the age of 13 and visited New York. He finally returned to England to act in musical comedies, before being whisked off to Broadway.

Jerry Springer Born in London, while his parents were en route to America as they fled the Holocaust.

Charlie Chaplin Born in London in 1889, Chaplin was a survivor of a Cockney orphanage. He performed as a dancer and singer in childhood and went to America in 1912 with the Fred Karno company, where film bosses spotted him. He left America in 1952 after being accused of harbouring Communist sympathies, and returned only once before he died 25 years later.

Stan Laurel From a family of entertainers, Arthur Stanley Jefferson was born in 1890 in Lancashire, England, and went to America as Charlie Chaplin's understudy in a Fred Karno company tour. Instead of returning to England in 1912 with the rest of the company, he stayed in the USA to play vaudeville, before finally teaming up with rotund comedian Oliver Hardy to forge the first Hollywood film comedy team.

Zsa Zsa Gabor Born in Budapest, she became a teenage Miss Hungary before moving to the US in 1941. Better known for the number of men she married than her acting ability, Gabor became one of the most glamorous and witty women on TV.

HORSE TRIALS

The Pony Express, founded in 1860, cut weeks off the delivery of mail travelling between the east and west coasts. Small, lightweight horsemen were employed to gallop for 100km (60 mile) stretches with frequent horse swaps, so that letters whistled along at a rate of some 300km (190 miles) per day. Fastest in the saddle was Buffalo Bill Cody, who rode 515km (322 miles) in less than a day, on the backs of no fewer than 21 horses. It was a revelation for folks who had previously had to wait for mail to be delivered by a combination of boat and mule, during a two-month time period. However, despite its success, the Pony Express lasted for only 19 months. Its demise was signalled by the inauguration of a transcontinental telegraph system in 1861.

WOMAN WITH BULLS

America's first female bullfighter was Patricia McCormick, who, in January 1957, entered the bullring in Ciudad, Juárez, Mexico.

STATES IN SONG

David Ackles	'Oh California'
The Amboy Dukes	'Mississippi Murderer'
The Beach Boys	'California Girls'
Black Oak Arkansas	'The Hills Of Arkansas'
	'When Electricity Came To Kansas'
JJ Cale	'Louisiana Women'
	'Mississippi River'
Johnny Cash	'Tennessee Stud'
Ray Charles	'Georgia On My Mind'
Neil Diamond	'Kentucky Woman'
The Doors	'Alabama Song (Whiskey Bar)'
The Eagles	'Hotel California'
Steve Earle	'West Nashville Boogie'
Jerry Garcia	'Mississippi Moon'
Woody Guthrie	'Oregon Trail'
	'Washington Talkin' Blues'
Emmylou Harris	'Montana Cowgirl'
Skip James	'Illinois Blues'
Lynyrd Skynyrd	'Sweet Home Alabama'
Mamas And The Papas	'California Dreamin''
Willie Nelson	'Moonlight In Vermont'
	'City Of New Orleans'
Elvis Presley	'Hawaiian Sunset'
Otis Redding	'Tennessee Waltz'
The Rolling Stones	'Sweet Virginia'
Simon And Garfunkel	'The Only Living Boy In New York'
Nina Simone	'Mississippi Goddam'
Frank Sinatra	'New York, New York'
Bruce Springsteen	'Streets Of Philadelphia'
	'Nebraska'
George Thorogood	'Oklahoma Sweetheart'
Stevie Ray Vaughan	'Texas Flood'
Slim Whitman	'Tennessee Waltz'
Neil Young	'The Emperor Of Wyoming'

MONEY WORRIES

When Hetty Green died in 1916 at the age of 80, she left a fortune worth more than $100 million (£60 million). She was an heiress, who compounded her fortune by wheeling and dealing on the stock market. Yet despite her riches, miserly Hetty refused to visit restaurants and, to save cash, survived on a diet of broken biscuits and oatmeal. She lived in a two-roomed furnished apartment instead of a penthouse or hotel, and dressed in rags. When she consulted a doctor in her later years, Hetty produced money to settle the consultation fee from an aged handbag that was tied around her waist with string.

THE COST OF WAR

During the 18 months that America spent at war before the Armistice of 1918, more than 116,500 US military personnel lost their lives – less than 3 per cent of the total of 4,355,000 Americans fighting for the Allies. The losses, although tragic, compare well to the death tolls of individual battles that took place before 1917. In 1914, in the first battle of Ypres, 250,000 died, while in the 1916 Battle of the Somme (which raged between July and November), more than 1,000,000 perished.

CITIES IN SONG

The Byrds	'Tulsa Country'
	'Mae Jean Goes To Hollywood'
Glen Campbell	'Galveston'
	'By the Time I Get To Phoenix'
Crosby Stills Nash And Young	'Woodstock'
Fats Domino	'Detroit City Blues'
Eminem	'Say Goodbye Hollywood'
Ella Fitzgerald	'Manhattan'
Leadbelly	'Fort Worth And Dallas Blues'
Little Feat	'Oh Atlanta'
Dean Martin	'Houston'
Nancy Sinatra	'Jackson'
Steely Dan	'East St Louis Toodle-oo'
Velvet Underground	'Coney Island Steeplechase'
Tom Waits	'San Diego Serenade'
ZZ Top	'Just Left Chicago'
	'Heaven, Hell Or Houston'

ITALIAN JOB

Irving Berlin was paid just 37c (22p) for the first song he published – 'Marie From Sunny Italy'.

HOT WATER

The water in the fountain of South Dakota's Capitol Building contains so much sulphur that it can be burned, thus creating the so-called 'flaming fountain'.

TORPEDO SINKS PEACE

When the Cunard liner *Lusitania* – travelling from New York to Liverpool – was sunk off the Irish coast by a German U-boat on 7 May 1915, nearly 130 American lives were among the 1,200 dead, including millionaire yachtsman Alfred Vanderbilt and other personal friends of President Woodrow Wilson. This single act sparked riots in New York and threatened a carefully wrought US policy of neutrality during World War I, although it was two years before America finally joined the conflict for the purposes of saving democracy. When American soldiers later fought in the trenches, they rallied one another with the cry of 'Remember the *Lusitania*'.

ARNOLD SCHWARZENEGGER VERSUS SYLVESTER STALLONE

	Schwarzenegger	**Stallone**
Aka	Arnie	Sly
Born	30 July 1947 in Graz, Austria	6 July 1946 in New York
Height	188cm (6ft 2in)	175cm (5ft 9in)
Film successes	*Conan The Barbarian*	*Rocky (I–V)*
	Terminator (I–III)	*Rambo (I–III)*
	Kindergarten Cop	

What's the connection? They became business partners in the Planet Hollywood enterprise.

For the future: Arnie was elected Governor of California in October 2003, while Sly is likely to reprise his most famous roles.

What Arnie said about Sly: 'It's a shame no one taught him to be cool… There's nothing that anyone can do out there to save his ass and his image.'

What Sly said about Arnie: 'I'd like to skip rope with his entrails.'

WEDDING WHISKERS

Amish men shave until they marry, then they grow a beard.

STARS WHO HAD GOOD REASON TO CHANGE THEIR NAMES

Alan Alda (from Alphonso D'Abruzzo)
Fred Astaire (from Frederick Austerlitz)
Charles Bronson (from Charles Buchinski)
Yul Brynner (from Taijde Khan)
Bobby Darin (from Walden Robert Cassotto)
Doris Day (from Doris von Kappelhoff)
John Denver (from Henry John Deutschendorf Jr)
Marlene Dietrich (from Maria Magdalene von Losch)
John Garfield (from Julius Garfinkle)
Judy Garland (from Frances Gumm)
James Garner (from James Scott Baumgardner)
Rock Hudson (from Roy Scherer)
Al Jolson (from Asa Yoelson)
Walter Matthau (from Walter Matuschanskavasky)
Robert Taylor (from Spangler Arlington Brugh)
Tina Turner (from Annie Mae Bullock)
John Wayne (from Marion Michael Morrison)
Harpo, Groucho, Chico, Gummo and Zeppo Marx (from Arthur, Julius, Leonard, Milton and Herbert Marx)

TEN-DOLLAR MAN

The man featured on the US $10 bill is Alexander Hamilton, who became the first US Secretary of the Treasury under President Washington and was later killed by Vice-President Aaron Burr. In the 1800 election, Burr and Thomas Jefferson, both competing for the presidency, had 73 votes each. Eventually the presidency went to Jefferson and many believed that Hamilton's political mudslinging might have cost Burr the election. Animosity between the two men came to a head in 1804, when Burr challenged Hamilton to a duel. Hamilton accepted and was mortally wounded on 11 July. Despite talk of murder charges, no indictment was laid against Aaron Burr, although he was later charged with treason after an attempt to establish his own empire in the south.

GRAMMY AWARDS – ALBUM OF THE YEAR

Year	Album	Artist
1958	*The Music From Peter Gunn*	Henry Mancini
1959	*Come Dance With Me*	Frank Sinatra
1960	*Button Down Mind*	Bob Newhart
1961	*Judy At Carnegie Hall*	Judy Garland
1962	*The First Family*	Vaughn Meader
1963	*The Barbra Streisand Album*	Barbra Streisand
1964	*Getz/Gilberto*	Stan Getz/João Gilberto
1965	*September Of My Years*	Frank Sinatra
1966	*Sinatra, A Man And His Music*	Frank Sinatra
1967	*Sergeant Pepper's Lonely Hearts Club Band*	The Beatles
1968	*By The Time I Get To Phoenix*	Glen Campbell
1969	*Blood Sweat And Tears*	Blood Sweat And Tears
1970	*Bridge Over Troubled Water*	Simon And Garfunkel
1971	*Tapestry*	Carole King
1972	*The Concert For Bangladesh*	George Harrison/ Ravi Shankar/Bob Dylan
1973	*Innervisions*	Stevie Wonder
1974	*Fulfillingness' First Finale*	Stevie Wonder
1975	*Still Crazy After All These Years*	Paul Simon
1976	*Songs In The Key Of Life*	Stevie Wonder
1977	*Rumours*	Fleetwood Mac
1978	*Saturday Night Fever*	The Bee Gees and others
1979	*52nd Street*	Billy Joel
1980	*Christopher Cross*	Christopher Cross
1981	*Double Fantasy*	John Lennon/Yoko Ono
1982	*Toto IV*	Toto
1983	*Thriller*	Michael Jackson
1984	*Can't Slow Down*	Lionel Richie
1985	*No Jacket Required*	Phil Collins
1986	*Graceland*	Paul Simon
1987	*The Joshua Tree*	U2
1988	*Faith*	George Michael
1989	*Nick Of Time*	Bonnie Raitt
1990	*Back On The Block*	Quincy Jones
1991	*Unforgettable*	Natalie Cole
1992	*Unplugged*	Eric Clapton
1993	*The Bodyguard*	Whitney Houston
1994	*Unplugged*	Tony Bennett

1995	*Jagged Little Pill*	Alanis Morissette
1996	*Falling Into You*	Celine Dion
1997	*Time Out Of Mind*	Bob Dylan
1998	*The Miseducation Of Lauryn Hill*	Lauryn Hill
1999	*Supernatural*	Santana
2000	*Two Against Nature*	Steely Dan
2001	*O Brother Where Art Thou?*	Various artists (soundtrack)
2002	*Come Away With Me*	Norah Jones

SIGNATORIES OF THE DECLARATION OF INDEPENDENCE

Connecticut	Oliver Wolcott, Roger Sherman, Samuel Huntington, William Williams
Delaware	Caesar Rodney, George Read, Thomas McKean
Georgia	Button Gwinnett, George Walton, Lyman Hall
Maryland	Samuel Chase, William Paca, Thomas Stone, Charles Carrol
Massachusetts	John Hancock, Samuel Adams, John Adams, Robert Treat Paine, Elbridge Gerry
New Hampshire	Josiah Bartlett, William Whipple, Matthew Thornton
New Jersey	Richard Stockton, John Witherspoon, Francis Hopkinson, John Hart, Abraham Clark
New York	William Floyd, Philip Livingston, Francis Lewis, Lewis Morris
North Carolina	William Hooper, Joseph Hewes, John Penn
Pennsylvania	Robert Morris, Benjamin Rush, Benjamin Franklin, John Morton, George Clymer, James Smith, George Taylor, James Wilson, George Ross
Rhode Island	Stephen Hopkins, William Ellery
South Carolina	Edward Rutledge, Thomas Heyward, Thomas Lynch, Arthur Middleton
Virginia	George Wythe, Richard Henry Lee, Thomas Jefferson, Benjamin Harrison, Thomas Nelson Jr, Carter Braxton, Francis Lightfoot Lee

YOUR BET, SUCKER

Poker strategy lies in the DNA of most Americans, but they should never forget the valuable advice of Amarillo Slim – aka Thomas Austin Preston Jnr of Amarillo, Texas – a successful pro-gambler for more than 50 years. Slim, a former poker World Series champion, has won pots 'bigger'n a show dog could jump over'. Asked the secret of his success, he once replied, 'If you don't see a sucker at the table, it's you.'

AMERICAN BILLIONAIRES

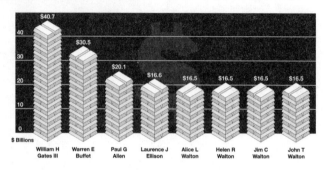

A COLLECTION OF STRANGE STATEMENTS MADE BY GEORGE W BUSH

'When I was coming up, it was a dangerous world, and you knew exactly who they were. It was us versus them, and it was clear who them was. Today we are not so sure who the they are, but we know they're there.'
Speaking at Iowa Western Community College, 12 January 2000

'I think anybody who doesn't think I'm smart enough to handle the job is underestimating me.'
US News & World Report, 3 April 2000

'As governor of Texas, I have set high standards for our public schools and I have met those standards.'
Speaking on CNN, 30 August 2000

'The best way to relieve families from time is to let them keep some of their own money.'
Speaking at Westminster, California, 13 September 2000

'I understand small business growth, I was one.'
New York Daily News, 19 September 2000

'More and more of our imports come from overseas.'
Speaking at Beaverton, Oregon, 25 September 2000

'I know the human being and fish can coexist peacefully.'
Speaking at Saginaw, Michigan, 29 September 2000

'I think we all agree, the past is over.'
Dallas Morning News, 10 May 2000

AN ALPHABET OF UNDERWORLD SPEAK

all on top: there's no truth in it

angel: supplier of money for a proposed crime

angle: to make money under false pretences

apple: victim of a crime

Arctic explorer: drug addict; commonly a cocaine user

back gate discharge: death of a convict in prison; coffin leaves by a back gate

bag: to imprison

bagman: distributor of stolen cash

band-house: antiquated term for US prison

bee on (put the): to blame

belch: to inform, and sometimes a reference to an informer

bend: to murder

bent: addicted to criminal activity

big house: prison

bomb: large sum of cash

boodle: fake currency

boost: shoplift

bottle and stopper: policeman

box: bank safe

broadsman: card-sharp

bugs: mad, crazy

bull: prison warder

bunny: victim of a confidence trickster

burn: to electrocute, kill or cheat

can: prison

canary: informer, grass

chatterbox: machine gun

chill off: to kill

choke: bribe

chopper: Thompson machine gunman

clean: free from suspicion

clip: to burgle or rob

cold deck: to adulterate cards from a clean deck of cards

con: convict

creepers: soft shoes

dead: reformed criminal

deck: small packet; usually containing drugs

derrick: shoplifter

deuce: two-year prison sentence

dip: pickpocket

AN ALPHABET OF UNDERWORLD SPEAK (CONT'D)

drop: predetermined point for the disposal of stolen goods
elbow: pickpocket's accomplice
eye: private investigator
faker: petty swindler
fall: funds put aside by criminals for expected legal fees
finger: act of betrayal by criminal to police
finishing school: female prison
fish: convict
fix: to bribe
flatty: US policeman
frame: act of an innocent person being made to look guilty
glass: diamonds
gofor: an easily duped person
gorilla: violent criminal
gow: alternative reference for opium
green: manufacture of counterfeit monies
H: heroin
handful: five-year prison sentence
harness bull: uniformed police officer
heat: police pressure
heist: robbery
hit the grit: jump from a moving train or other vehicle
hole up: go into hiding
hood: racketeer, criminal
hop: opium; general reference for drugs
houseman: burglar
housework: burglary
hustle: general term for criminal activity
ice: diamonds
jack-roll: act of robbing a drunken person
jimmy: force with a crowbar or jemmy
jolt: sentence of imprisonment
jug: bank safe
kite: worthless cheque
lamp: look, observe
lifeboat: a reprieve
lighthouse: a lookout man
magazine: six-month sentence
moll-buzzer: pickpocket devoting his crime to women
mouthpiece: police informer

nix: warning word
obey: post office
paper hanger: forger
pigeon: to inform to the police
pogey: county jail
raincheck: commutation of a long sentence or death sentence
rap: accusation or charge
rod: revolver
sawyer: sawn-off shotgun
score: proceeds of theft
scrip: cheque or money that is forged
shelf: pawnshop
sing: confess, inform
sleep: prison sentence
smoke: act of shooting somebody
sneeze: act of informing to police
snow: cocaine
space: a year's prison sentence
spring: release from prison via an escape
squeal: act of informing police
stir: prison
stool pigeon: paid informer
tea: marijuana
ticket: convict and send to prison
trigger man: assassin, professional killer
typewriter: Tommy gun
ukulele: drum from a Tommy gun
velvet: illicitly gained money
wooden kimono: coffin
yip: to complain
zebra: prison clothing
zoo: jail or prison

GLUE-LETTER DAY

Adhesive stamps were introduced in the United States on 31 March 1918.

SPOUTING OFF

There are more geysers in Yellowstone National Park than in all the rest of the world put together.

PUNTING FOR THE BIG ONE

The most audacious betting coup in US history is arguably the Breeders' Cup scandal of October 2002, when a punter called Derrick Davis picked all six winners on the card to scoop $3 million (£1.8 million) from a $12 (£7.25) stake. Davis never collected his prize because an investigation revealed how an accomplice working for a national bet-processing company substituted his selections with names of the winning nags. This was possible because of a delay between bets being placed at off-track bookmakers and registered on the database at Arlington Park, Illinois, where the race is run. Davis initially put it all down to luck, but later changed his plea. He was jailed for three years.

WISE WORDS INDEED

A dozen lines that Bart writes on the blackboard in the opening credits of *The Simpsons:*

'Hillbillies are people too'
'I am not a licensed hairstylist'
'I am not the new Dalai Lama'
'Silly string is not a nasal spray'
'I cannot absolve sins'
'There was no Roman god named Fartacus'
'A trained ape could not teach gym'
'No one wants to hear from my armpits'
'Ralph won't morph if you squeeze him hard enough'
'I will not encourage others to fly'
'Teacher is not a leper'
'No one wants to hear about my sciatica'

US STATES AND CAPITALS

State	Capital
Alabama	Montgomery
Alaska	Juneau
Arizona	Phoenix
Arkansas	Little Rock
California	Sacramento
Colorado	Denver
Connecticut	Hartford
Delaware	Dover
Florida	Tallahassee

Georgia	Atlanta
Hawaii	Honolulu
Idaho	Boise
Illinois	Springfield
Indiana	Indianapolis
Iowa	Des Moines
Kansas	Topeka
Kentucky	Frankfurt
Louisiana	Baton Rouge
Maine	Augusta
Maryland	Annapolis
Massachusetts	Boston
Michigan	Lansing
Minnesota	St Paul
Mississippi	Jackson
Missouri	Jefferson City
Montana	Helena
Nebraska	Lincoln
Nevada	Carson City
New Hampshire	Concord
New Jersey	Trenton
New Mexico	Santa Fe
New York	Albany
North Carolina	Raleigh
North Dakota	Bismarck
Ohio	Columbus
Oklahoma	Oklahoma City
Oregon	Salem
Pennsylvania	Harrisburg
Rhode Island	Providence
South Carolina	Columbia
South Dakota	Pierre
Tennessee	Nashville
Texas	Austin
Utah	Salt Lake City
Vermont	Montpelier
Virginia	Richmond
Washington	Olympia
West Virginia	Charleston
Wisconsin	Madison
Wyoming	Cheyenne

WHEELS OF FORTUNE

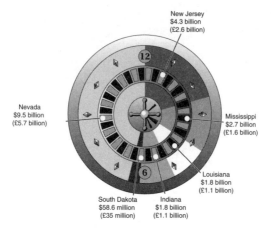

New Jersey
$4.3 billion
(£2.6 billion)

Nevada
$9.5 billion
(£5.7 billion)

Mississippi
$2.7 billion
(£1.6 billion)

Louisiana
$1.8 billion
(£1.1 billion)

South Dakota
$58.6 million
(£35 million)

Indiana
$1.8 billion
(£1.1 billion)

Only 11 US states allow commercial casinos, and no prizes for guessing which one is undisputed King of the Wheel.

LET'S TOSS FOR IT

If you're a high roller, or 'whale' as they say in Las Vegas casinos, you think nothing of dropping millions a night on the green baize. The Australian media billionaire Kerry Packer once reportedly took the MGM Grand for $26 million (£15.7 million), playing six hands of blackjack for $200,000 (£120,000) per hand. However, Packer's finest hour came as he was sitting in another Vegas casino as an attractive girl was being loudly seduced by a boastful Texan oilman. The story goes that an irritated Packer eventually leaned across to ask mildly how much the American was worth.

'$100 million [£62 million],' cried the man.

'Tell you what,' suggested Packer, smoothly. 'I'll toss you for it.'

SAD DAY

In 1862, Abraham Lincoln instituted the first income-tax law in American history.

SOME PATRIOTIC FILM TITLES

American Beauty
American Gigolo
American Graffiti
American Pie
The American Success Company
An American Tail

An American Tragedy
An American Werewolf In London
Independence Day
Made In America
The Secret Life Of An American Wife

STONE ME

The world's largest hailstone, which fell on Potter, Nebraska, on 6 July 1928, was 43cm (17in) in diameter.

BRIGHT SPARK

In 1902, Topsy the elephant killed her keeper, JF Blount, at Coney Island when he tried to feed her a lit cigarette. Using her trunk, she scooped him up and hurled him to the ground. A crowd of 1,500 people gathered at the same venue to watch Topsy's electrocution on 5 January 1903.

THE WIT AND WISDOM OF DOROTHY PARKER (1893–1967)

'I'm never going to be famous. I don't do anything, not one single thing. I used to bite my nails, but I don't even do that any more.'

'People are more fun than anybody.'

After hearing that Calvin Coolidge had died: 'How could they tell?'

In a book review: 'This is not a novel to be tossed aside lightly. It should be thrown aside with great force.'

'Brevity is the soul of lingerie.'

'I like to have a Martini, two at the very most. After three I'm under the table, after four I'm under my host!'

'Men seldom make passes at girls who wear glasses.'

In a review of a play starring Katharine Hepburn: 'Miss Hepburn runs the gamut of emotions from A to B.'

CHRONOLOGY OF THE DOW'S ROAD TO 10,000

26 May 1896 Charles Dow launches index at 40.94 points. The DJIA then had only 12 stocks

12 January 1906 Index closes at 100.25, the first close above 100.

28–29 October 1929 Stock market crashes at 12.82 per cent and 11.73 per cent back to back (38.33 and 30.57 points), and ushers in the Great Depression.

12 March 1956 First close above 500, at 500.24. Trading on the New York Stock Exchange totals 766 million shares for the year.

8 February 1971 NASDAQ Stock Market is born.

14 November 1972 Dow's first close above 1,000, called Wall Street's equivalent of breaking the sound barrier. The index briefly reached 1,000 in early 1966, but retreated and closed below that milestone.

12 August 1982 Birth of the long-term bull market.

8 January 1987 First close above 2,000 at 2,002.25.

19 October 1987 Black Monday crash of record at 22.61 per cent (508 points).

11 October 1990 Commonly recognised start of current bull market.

21 November 1995 DJIA has first-ever close above 5,000 nine months after hitting 4,000.

26 May 1996 Centennial of DJIA is celebrated.

16 July 1997 The Dow Jones index closes above 8,000. In less than two and a half years, the Dow Jones has managed to double in size.

27–28 October 1997 Biggest ever point loss at 554.26 (but only 7.18 per cent of Dow's total value), followed by then-biggest point gain: 337.17 (4.71 per cent).

8 September 1998 Biggest-ever point gain at 380.53 (4.98 per cent), after seven weeks of declines on global economic turmoil.

29 March 1999 DJIA jumps 184.54 (1.88 per cent) to 10,006.78 primarily behind tech-stock rally.

Source: *Wall Street Journal*, 30 March 1999

SPACE EXPLORATION TIMELINE

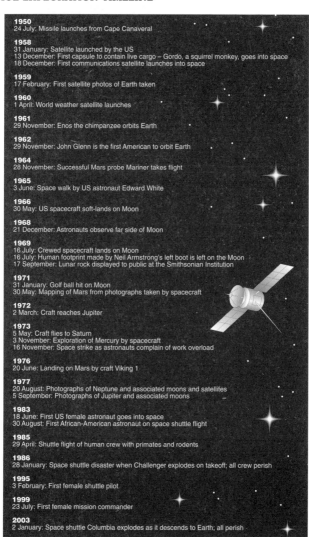

1950
24 July: Missile launches from Cape Canaveral

1958
31 January: Satellite launched by the US
13 December: First capsule to contain live cargo – Gordo, a squirrel monkey, goes into space
18 December: First communications satellite launches into space

1959
17 February: First satellite photos of Earth taken

1960
1 April: World weather satellite launches

1961
29 November: Enos the chimpanzee orbits Earth

1962
29 November: John Glenn is the first American to orbit Earth

1964
28 November: Successful Mars probe Mariner takes flight

1965
3 June: Space walk by US astronaut Edward White

1966
30 May: US spacecraft soft-lands on Moon

1968
21 December: Astronauts observe far side of Moon

1969
16 July: Crewed spacecraft lands on Moon
16 July: Human footprint made by Neil Armstrong's left boot is left on the Moon
17 September: Lunar rock displayed to public at the Smithsonian Institution

1971
31 January: Golf ball hit on Moon
30 May: Mapping of Mars from photographs taken by spacecraft

1972
2 March: Craft reaches Jupiter

1973
5 May: Craft flies to Saturn
3 November: Exploration of Mercury by spacecraft
16 November: Space strike as astronauts complain of work overload

1976
20 June: Landing on Mars by craft Viking 1

1977
20 August: Photographs of Neptune and associated moons and satellites
5 September: Photographs of Jupiter and associated moons

1983
18 June: First US female astronaut goes into space
30 August: First African-American astronaut on space shuttle flight

1985
29 April: Shuttle flight of human crew with primates and rodents

1986
28 January: Space shuttle disaster when Challenger explodes on takeoff; all crew perish

1995
3 February: First female shuttle pilot

1999
23 July: First female mission commander

2003
2 January: Space shuttle Columbia explodes as it descends to Earth; all perish

THINGS THEY PROBABLY WISH THEY HADN'T SAID...

'I'm glad he's dead. Now I'm the King.'
Jerry Lee Lewis, after hearing Elvis was dead

'I did not have sexual relations with that woman.'
Bill Clinton on Monica Lewinsky

'Only the little people pay taxes.'
Leona Helmsley during a tax evasion scandal

'There will be no whitewash at the White House.'
Richard Nixon, speaking on national television at the height of the Watergate crisis in 1973

'A child needs more love and affection than you can get in a large family.'
Mia Farrow, one of seven children, now the mother of 4 naturally conceived and 11 adopted children

'The watertight subdivision of the *Olympic* and *Titanic* is very complete, and is so arranged that any two main compartments may be flooded without in any way involving the safety of the ship.'
A 1911 copy of the *Shipbuilder*

'Outside of the killings, Washington has one of the lowest crime rates in the country.'
Marion Barry, Mayor of Washington, DC

'I've never had major knee surgery on any other part of my body.'
Winston Bennett, University of Kentucky basketball forward

'I believe that mink are raised for being turned into fur coats and if we didn't wear fur coats those little animals would never have been born. So is it better not to have been born or to have lived for a year or two to have been turned into a fur coat? I don't know.'
Barbi Benton, former *Playboy* bunny

'You can observe a lot by watching.'
Yogi Berra

'Sure, it's going to kill a lot of people, but they may be dying of something else anyway.'
Othal Brand, member of a Texas pesticide review board

'They were doing a full back shot of me in a swimsuit and I thought, Oh my God, I have to be so brave. See, every woman hates herself from behind.'
Cindy Crawford, supermodel

'We got married because we love each other and we decided to make a life together. We are heterosexual and monogamous and take our commitment to each other very seriously. There is not and never has been a pre-nuptial agreement of any kind. Reports of a divorce are totally false. There are no plans, nor have there ever been any plans for divorce. We remain very married.'
A personal statement by **Richard Gere** and **Cindy Crawford**, published in *The Times* on 6 May 1994, a year before the couple divorced

'There are not enough Indians in the world to defeat the Seventh Cavalry.'
George Armstrong Custer

'He didn't say that. He was reading what was given to him in a speech.'
Richard Darman, director of OMB, explaining why President Bush wasn't following up on his campaign pledge that there would be no loss of wetlands

'I haven't committed a crime. What I did was fail to comply with the law.'
David Dinkins, New York City Mayor, answering accusations that he failed to pay his taxes

YOUNG BRAVES

The Medal of Honor is the United States' highest military honour, and is given for military heroism 'above and beyond the call of duty'. Five American Indians were awarded the Medal of Honor in the 20th century:

• Jack C. Montgomery – a Cherokee from Oklahoma
• Ernest Childers – a Creek from Oklahoma
• Van Barfoot – a Chocktaw from Mississippi
• Mitchell Red Cloud Jr – a Winnebago from Wisconsin (posthumous)
• Charles George – a Cherokee from North Carolina (posthumous)

Twenty medals of 'honour' were awarded to US soldiers for their part in the Massacre at Wounded Knee, on 29 December 1890, which resulted in the death of over 300 Lakota Sioux men, women and children.

DOGGONE

The Boston terrier is the only breed of dog developed in the US.

DARK DAYS

For the first 19 years that Crayola crayons were produced, they came in only one colour – black.

HOW NOW DOW

Charles Dow first published the Dow Jones Industrial Average on 26 May 1896 as a new way of measuring economic might and performance. At the time it consisted of a dozen stocks relating to the agricultural and raw materials arena. Back then, the *Customers Afternoon Letter*, a forerunner of the *Wall Street Journal*, published the closing prices of 12 stock prices: those of American Cotton Oil, American Sugar, American Tobacco, Chicago Gas, Distilling & Cattle Feeding, General Electric, Laclede Gas, National Lead, North American, Tennessee Coal & Iron, US Leather Preferred and US Rubber.

Only one of the first 12 appears in the Average today: General Electric. It also lost its niche for a while when it was deleted in 1898, but made a comeback nine years later, usurping Tennessee Coal & Iron.

Today the Dow Jones Industrial Average (DJIA) is the flagship of industrial indicators. The index is now made up of the share prices of 30 major US corporations, most of them traded on the New York Stock Exchange (NYSE). The value measured by the Dow Jones grew to more than 10,000 points, although the figure was knocked back by uncertainty created following the terrorist attacks of 9/11.

THE PULITZER PRIZE

Conceived by the American publisher Joseph Pulitzer in 1917, it is given each year in recognition of outstanding contributions to American journalism, literature and music. The Pulitzer prize for fiction has gone to:

1918	Ernest Poole	*His Family*
1919	Booth Tarkington	*The Magnificent Ambersons*
1920	No award this year	
1921	Edith Wharton	*The Age Of Innocence*
1922	Booth Tarkington	*Alice Adams*
1923	Willa Cather	*One Of Ours*
1924	Margaret Wilson	*The Able McLaughlins*
1925	Edna Ferber	*So Big*
1926	Sinclair Lewis	*Arrowsmith*
1927	Louis Bromfield	*Early Autumn*
1928	Thornton Wilder	*The Bridge At San Luis Rey*
1929	Julia Peterkin	*Scarlet Sister Mary*
1930	Oliver LaFarge	*Laughing Boy*
1931	Margaret Ayer Barnes	*Years Of Grace*
1932	Pearl S Buck	*The Good Earth*

1933	TS Stribling	*The Store*
1934	Caroline Miller	*Lamb In His Bosom*
1935	Josephine Winslow Johnson	*Now in November*
1936	Harold L Davis	*Honey In The Horn*
1937	Margaret Mitchell	*Gone With The Wind*
1938	John Phillips Marquand	*The Late George Apley*
1939	Marjorie Kinnan Rawlings	*The Yearling*
1940	John Steinbeck	*The Grapes Of Wrath*
1941	No award this year (originally given to Ernest Hemingway for *For Whom The Bell Tolls*, but vetoed by the prize committee)	
1942	Ellen Glasgow	*In This Our Life*
1943	Upton Sinclair	*Dragon's Teeth*
1944	Martin Flavin	*Journey In The Dark*
1945	John Hersey	*A Bell For Adano*
1946	No award this year	
1947	Robert Penn Warren	*All The King's Men*
1948	James A Michener	*Tales Of The South Pacific*
1949	James Gould Cozzens	*Guard Of Honor*
1950	AB Guthrie Jr	*The Way West*
1951	Conrad Richter	*The Town*
1952	Herman Wouk	*The Caine Mutiny*
1953	Ernest Hemingway	*The Old Man And The Sea*
1954	No award this year	
1955	William Faulkner	*A Fable*
1956	Mackinley Kantor	*Andersonville*
1957	No award this year	
1958	James Agee	*A Death In The Family*
1959	Robert Lewis Taylor	*The Travels Of Jamie McPheeters*
1960	Allen Drury	*Advise And Consent*
1961	Harper Lee	*To Kill A Mockingbird*
1962	Edwin O'Connor	*The Edge Of Sadness*
1963	William Faulkner	*The Reivers*
1964	No award this year	
1965	Shirley Ann Grau	*The Keepers Of The House*
1966	Katherine Anne Porter	*The Collected Stories Of Katherine Anne Porter*
1967	Bernard Malamud	*The Fixer*
1968	William Styron	*The Confessions Of Nat Turner*
1969	N Scott Momaday	*House Made Of Dawn*
1970	Jean Stafford	*Collected Stories*
1971	No award this year	
1972	Wallace Stegner	*Angle Of Repose*

THE PULITZER PRIZE (CONT'D)

1973	Eudora Welty	*The Optimist's Daughter*
1974	No award this year	
1975	Michael Shaara	*The Killer Angels*
1976	Saul Bellow	*Humboldt's Gift*
1977	No award this year	
1978	James Alan McPherson	*Elbow Room*
1979	John Cheever	*The Stories Of John Cheever*
1980	Norman Mailer	*The Executioner's Song*
1981	John Kennedy Toole	*A Confederacy Of Dunces*
1982	John Updike	*Rabbit Is Rich*
1983	Alice Walker	*The Color Purple*
1984	William Kennedy	*Ironweed*
1985	Alison Lurie	*Foreign Affairs*
1986	Larry McMurtry	*Lonesome Dove*
1987	Peter Taylor	*A Summons To Memphis*
1988	Toni Morrison	*Beloved*
1989	Anne Tyler	*Breathing Lessons*
1990	Oscar Hijuelos	*The Mambo Kings Play Songs Of Love*
1991	John Updike	*Rabbit At Rest*
1992	Jane Simley	*A Thousand Acres*
1993	Robert Olen Butler	*A Good Scent From A Strange Mountain*
1994	E Annie Proulx	*The Shipping News*
1995	Carol Shields	*The Stone Diaries*
1996	Richard Ford	*Independence Day*
1997	Steven Millhauser	*Martin Dressler: The Tale Of An American Dreamer*
1998	Philip Roth	*American Pastoral*
1999	Michael Cunningham	*The Hours*
2000	Jhumpa Lahiri	*Interpreter Of Maladies*
2001	Michael Chabon	*The Amazing Adventures of Kavalier And Clay*
2002	Richard Russo	*Empire Falls*
2003	Jeffrey Eugenides	*Middlesex*

NAME FAME

One out of every 144 people in America has the last name of Smith.

21ST-CENTURY CENTURIONS

Although her birth certificate was lost in a house fire, friends and supporters of Mary Thompson of Shelby, Mississippi, claimed her age was 119 years 69 days when she died on 10 October 2001. In life she presumed her longevity was down to generous quantities of Crown Royal and Juicy Fruit chewing gum. Two months before her death a British TV station recorded her wishing the Queen Mother a happy 101st birthday.

Meanwhile, Maud Farris-Luse of Michigan believed she had achieved a ripe old age through her liking for boiled dandelion greens and fried fish. Born in 1887, she was first wed in 1903, and it is this marriage certificate that verified her age. Widowed in 1951, she married for a second time, but her husband survived for just three years. Indeed, by the time of her death in March 2002, aged 115, she outlived all but one of her seven children.

Born in Minnesota in 1888, Delvina Dahlheimer lived for 113 years and 72 days. This means she was 11 at the turn of the 20th century, 30 at the end of World War I, and almost 75 when President Kennedy was shot. Her death in Elk River came on 13 March 2002.

THE (B)RAT PACK

Rat Pack
The main men in the rat pack were Frank Sinatra, Dean Martin, Sammy Davis Jr, Peter Lawford and Joey Bishop. They became famous for their charismatic singing performances at the Sands Hotel and Casino in Las Vegas, and were associated with a wild lust for life. Originally known as the Clan, the name was changed to remove its association with the racist Ku Klux Klan. Their unity was largely dissolved with Sinatra's acrimonious departure from the Sands. Friends and drinking partners of the Rat Pack included Humphrey Bogart, Lauren Bacall, Shirley MacLaine, Judy Garland, Tony Curtis, Kim Novak and John F Kennedy.

Brat Pack
A phrase used to sum up the most exciting young actors of the 1980s, who together turned out cult films such as *The Breakfast Club* and *St Elmo's Fire*. Membership of this elite group is often disputed, but it usually refers to Rob Lowe, Molly Ringwald, Anthony Michael Hall, Ally Sheedy, Emilio Estevez, Andrew McCarthy, Judd Nelson, Demi Moore, Matthew Broderick, John Cusack, Robert Downey Jr and Sean Penn.

ANALYSIS FEVER

There is one psychiatrist or psychologist for every 2,641 Americans.

CHILD STARS

Drew Barrymore

Although she was part of a famous acting dynasty, Barrymore exceeded all expectations when she starred in Steven Spielberg's *ET – The Extra Terrestrial*, made in 1982. Aged just 7, she turned in a magical performance. However, the spell was broken when she embarked on a destructive lifestyle of drink and drugs before adolescence. She managed to revive her career following rehab, emerging as a glamorous and successful adult star.

Macaulay Culkin

Beginning a showbiz career on the stage at 4, Culkin made his name at the age of 10 starring in *Home Alone* (1990), as an enterprising kid, forgotten by his family during the Christmas break, outwitting two burglars.

Deanna Durbin

Born in Canada but raised in California, sweet-faced Deanna Durbin began making films at 15, and her consummate talents helped to save Universal Studios from bankruptcy in the late 1930s.

Judy Garland

She cut her teeth in vaudeville before being signed to MGM by studio chief Louis B Mayer at the age of 13. A year later, she starred in her first film, *Pigskin Parade*. Aged 17, she achieved lasting fame for her performance as Dorothy in *The Wizard Of Oz*.

Tatum O'Neal

Daughter of *Love Story* star Ryan O'Neal, Tatum won an Oscar as Best Supporting Actress aged 10 in the film *Paper Moon*.

Mickey Rooney

Making his first stage appearance at 15 months, Rooney became part of a family act before playing in his first short film at the age of 6, playing a midget. There followed a succession of comedy shorts before he was signed to Universal when he was 12.

Brooke Shields

Following a modelling career launched when she was still in nappies, Brooke Shields found big-screen fame at the age of 11 after playing a child prostitute in the film *Pretty Baby*.

Elizabeth Taylor

Although she was born in Britain, her American parents moved back to the States before World War II, settling in Los Angeles. In 1942, at the age of 10, Taylor's startling good looks won her a role in a film called *There's One Born Every Minute*. The following year she was in *Lassie Come Home* and in 1944, aged 12, she made her name in *National Velvet*.

Shirley Temple

For her dancing skills, Temple was picked for a starring role in a short film before she reached the age of 4. At 6, she received a special Academy Award 'in grateful recognition of her outstanding contribution to screen entertainment during the year 1934'. By the age of 10 she was the top box-office attraction in Hollywood.

DOW JONES STOCKS (SEPTEMBER 2003)

3M	Exxon Mobil	Johnson & Johnson
Alcoa	General Electric	McDonald's
American Express	General Motors	Merck
AT&T	Home Depot	Microsoft
Boeing	Honeywell	Philip Morris
Caterpillar	Hewlett-Packard	Procter & Gamble
Citigroup	IBM	SBC Communications
Coca-Cola	Intel	United Technologies
DuPont	International Paper Company	Wal-Mart
Eastman Kodak	JP Morgan	Walt Disney

10 TOP SURFING BEACHES (IN NO PARTICULAR ORDER)

- Sunset Beach, North Shore, Oahu, Hawaii
- Makalawena Beach, Hawaii
- Hanauma Bay, Hawaii
- Cape Florida State Recreational Area, Florida
- Malibu Beach, Malibu, California
- Ocracoke Island, North California
- Kaanapali, Hawaii
- Black's Beach, San Diego
- Hanalei Bay, Hawaii
- Trestle San Clemente, California

IN 1637...

...one out of every four shops in New York City was a tavern.

THE US STANDS FOR...

Today, 'Uncle Sam' is a familiar nickname given to America or its government. However, the character was probably inspired by a meatpacker called Sam Wilson who worked in Troy, New York, during America's 1812 war with Britain. A man with numerous nephews and nieces, he was affectionately known as Uncle Sam and, when the letters 'US' for United States were stamped on his meat barrels and sent to American soldiers, it was said they had come from Uncle Sam. Once this notion had been suggested, it spread rapidly until everyone made the US/Uncle Sam connection.

Previous well-known characters Yankee Doodle and Brother Jonathan inspired cartoonists of the era. Usually Uncle Sam is depicted in cartoon form with long white hair, chin whiskers, a tail coat, tall hat and stripy trousers. His most enduring appearances have been finger-wagging on army recruiting posters designed by James Montgomery Flagg, widely used during the World Wars I and II.

CROSS-COUNTY CAR

The Packard was the first car to cross America under its own power in 1903. The journey took 52 days.

US DOLLAR

The dollar sign was originally equipped with two vertical lines (in fact, sometimes you still see it used that way). The two vertical lines represented a U superimposed over the S, which stand for 'US'. So the United States is the only country that incorporates its own name into its monetary symbol.

THE DRAMA SURROUNDING LINCOLN'S ASSASSINATION

- Lincoln had already been the subject of 82 assassination attempts before Booth killed him.

- He went to the Ford Theater to see a production of *Our American Cousin,* a comedy by Tom Taylor starring Laura Keene.

- Synchronised efforts to assassinate the secretary of state, William H Seward, and the vice president, Andrew Johnson, were bungled. Conspirator Lewis Paine took a knife to Seward, but his prey survived. A third man, George Atzerodt, charged with murdering Johnson, lost his nerve and went for a pub crawl around Washington instead.

- Booth, who was from a distinguished acting dynasty, arrived at the theatre for the task dressed in black, in theatrical make-up and with a false beard.

- Apart from the derringer that fired the fatal shot, Booth was also sporting two Colt revolvers and a knife tucked in his waistband.

- In leaping from the theatre box after shooting the president, Booth snagged his spur in a curtain and fell down, fracturing a leg bone. When Maryland doctor Samuel Mudd tended the patient's broken leg, he had no idea he was helping an infamous fugitive. Despite his ignorance the hapless doctor was sentenced to hard labour for life. However, he did contribute one well-remembered phrase to the language, aptly summing up his dilemma: 'My name is Mudd.'

- Lewis Paine, George Atzerodt, fellow plotter Sam Arnold, and Mary Surratt (at whose boarding house they hatched their plans) were all hanged on 7 July 1865 after being convicted of conspiracy.

- General Ulysses Grant, hero of the Union forces, had been invited to join the president at the theatre. A prior engagement made with his son in New Jersey probably saved his life.

SELECT GATHERING

The signatories of the Declaration of Independence comprised 26 lawyers, 8 merchants, 6 doctors, 7 farmers, 1 printer, 2 military men, 1 minister, 1 shoemaker, 1 sailor, 1 surveyor and 2 politicians. There were no women, no Native Americans and no African Americans involved.

GRAUMAN'S CHINESE THEATER

Sid Grauman built Grauman's Chinese Theater in Hollywood in 1926. It is not only famous for hosting premières, but also for the array of celebrity hand and footprints captured in cement outside. The list of stars immortalised there is mighty, but here are a few facts you might not know about the famous forecourt.

Non-humans who have made their mark

R2-D2 from the *Star Wars* films and his comrade C-3PO
Champion, Gene Autry's horse
Tony, Tom Mix's horse
Trigger, Roy Rogers' horse
Donald Duck

Stars who left something other than hand or footprints

Groucho Marx left a print of his cigar.
Betty Grable left an imprint of her famous legs
John Wayne planted his fist in wet cement
Al Jolson knelt down for posterity
Jimmy Durante left a nose print
Whoopi Goldberg left a record of her hair braids

Stars who went two by two (or more)

Douglas Fairbanks and Mary Pickford (30 April 1927)
Wallace Beery and Marie Dressler (31 January 1931)
Maurice Chevalier and Jeanette MacDonald (4 December 1934)
William Powell and Myrna Loy (20 October 1936)
Clark Gable and WS Van Dyke (20 January 1937)
Dick Powell and Joan Blondell (10 February 1937)
Tyrone Power and Loretta Young (31 May 1937)
Tony Martin and Alice Faye (20 March 1938)
Edgar Bergen and Charlie McCarthy (20 July 1938)
George Raft and Rosa Grauman (25 March 1940)
Robert Taylor and Barbara Stanwyck (11 June 1941)

Bud Abbott and Lou Costello (8 December 1941)
Henry Fonda, Rita Hayworth, Charles Laughton, Edward G Robinson and
Charles Boyer (24 July 1942)
Bob Hope and Dorothy Lamour (5 February 1943)
Private Joe Brain and Esther Williams (1 August 1944)
Sid Grauman and Gene Tierney (24 January 1946)
Rex Harrison and Irene Dunne (8 July 1946)
Richard Widmark and Charles Nelson (24 April 1949)
Gregory Peck and Anne Baxter (15 December 1949)
Oskar Werner and Hildegarde Neff (13 December 1951)
Donald O'Connor and his mum Effie O'Connor (25 February 1953)
Jane Russell and Marilyn Monroe (26 June 1953)
Yul Brynner and Deborah Kerr (22 March 1956)
Rock Hudson, George Stevens and Elizabeth Taylor (26 September 1956)
Paul Newman and Joanne Woodward (25 May 1963)
Jack Lemmon and Shirley MacLaine (29 June 1963)
Star Trek creator Gene Roddenberry and stars William Shatner, Leonard
Nimoy, DeForrest Kelley, James Doohan, Walter Koenig, Nichelle
Nichols and George Takei (5 December 1991)

10 SURF SONGS

'Catch A Wave'	The Beach Boys
'The Lonely Surfer'	Jack Nitzsche
'Ride The Wild Surf'	Jan and Dean
'Surf City'	Jan and Dean
'Surfer Girl'	The Beach Boys
'Surfer Joe'	The Surfaris
'Surfer Stomp'	The Marketts
'Surfin''	The Beach Boys
'Surfin' USA'	The Beach Boys
'Surfin' Bird'	The Trashmen

FILED

President Lincoln had a good organisation technique a century before the
personal organiser came along. He kept a special envelope on his desk
labelled 'When you can't find it anywhere else, look in this.'

COMIC BOOK HEROES

The following actors have played some of the best-known comic book characters:

Alicia Silverstone – Batgirl
George Clooney – Batman
Michael Keaton – Batman
Val Kilmer – Batman
Ben Affleck – Daredevil
Eric Bana – The Incredible Hulk
Nicolas Hammond – Spider-Man
Tobey Maguire – Spider-Man
Halle Berry – Storm
Helen Slater – Supergirl
Christopher Reeve – Superman
Hugh Jackman – Wolverine

HOMER SIMPSON

According to the phone directory, there are only 24 Homer Simpsons in the United States – 5 of them live in Tennessee, 3 in North Carolina, 2 in Ohio and 1 in each of Arkansas, California, Colorado, Florida, Illinois, Indiana, Iowa, Kentucky, Massachusetts, Mississippi, Pennsylvania, Utah, Virginia and Washington.

TECHNICALLY...

...George Washington was not America's first president, as that accolade goes to John Hanson. He was followed by Elias Boudinot, Thomas Mifflin, Richard Henry Lee, Nathan Gorham, Arthur St Clair and Cyrus Griffin, who all sat in the hot seat before Washington arrived. Of course, Washington was the first to be elected by the people; the others were elected directly by the Continental Congress.

FOUR FAMOUS NATIVE AMERICANS

Pocahontas (c. 1595–1617)

Daughter of Chief Powhatan, Pocahontas was a pivotal link between incoming whites and Native Americans. According to the famous story, she saved the life of Captain John Smith just as he was about to be killed on the orders of Powhatan. In 1613, Pocahontas was captured by Captain Samuel Argall, taken to Jamestown, and held as a hostage for English prisoners being held by her father. She was converted to Christianity, and in 1614 married a settler called John Rolfe. Two years later, Pocahontas travelled to England with her husband and was presented to the king and queen. She died as she started on a return trip to America, and is buried at Gravesend, England.

Cochise (c1815–74)

Chief of the Chiricahua group of Apache in Arizona, Cochise was friendly towards the whites until 1861, when some relations were unjustly hanged by US soldiers for a crime they did not commit. After this, he waged relentless war against the US Army. Admired for his courage, integrity and military skill, Cochise's friendship with Thomas Jeffords became the key to peace. After conciliation talks in 1872, he agreed to live on a reservation, which was to be created from his native territory. Cochise's people were removed to another reservation after his death.

Geronimo (c1829–1909)

Born in Arizona, Geronimo was leader of a Chiricahua group of the Apaches. As a youth he fought with – amongst others – Cochise and Victorio. When the Chiricahua Reservation was abolished in 1876 Geronimo led a group of followers into Mexico. However, he was captured and returned to the new reservation in New Mexico. In 1881, he escaped again and led raids in Arizona and Sonora, Mexico. He surrendered in 1883 and was returned to the reservation. Two years later he left again, and after almost a year of war he agreed to surrender, but at the last minute he fled. Late in 1886, Geronimo and the remainder of his forces surrendered to General Nelson Appleton Miles, and they were deported as prisoners of war (without their families) to Florida. After some time in prison in Alabama, Geronimo was placed under military confinement at Fort Sill, Oklahoma, where he eventually settled down, adopted Christianity, and became a farmer. He went on to appear at the St Louis World's Fair and took part in Theodore Roosevelt's inaugural procession.

Sitting Bull (c1831–90)

Sitting Bull was the Sioux leader in the battle of Little Bighorn, where George Custer and his men were defeated and killed in 1876. Along with some of his followers, he escaped to Canada. They returned (in 1881) with the promise of a pardon and settled on a reservation. In 1885, he appeared in Buffalo Bill's Wild West Show, but his campaigning days were not over. Still influential, Sitting Bull encouraged the Sioux to refuse to sell their lands. He was killed by Native American police on a charge of resisting arrest. Originally buried in North Dakota, his remains were removed to South Dakota in 1954.

WORDS OF WISDOM

In 1939, ex-First Lady Nancy Reagan was in a high-school play in which she had only one line: 'They ought to elect the First Lady and then let her husband be President.'

SUNSET STRIP

Sunset Strip is one of the most famous addresses in the US. But there's more to the Strip than neon signs and celebrity spotters. Here are ten things that you (probably) didn't know.

- Sunset Strip has been at the forefront of everyone's mind since the 1960s TV series *'77 Sunset Strip*. But few people recall that – apart from the tarmac – the star of the show was the instantly forgettable Efrem Zimbalist Jr.

- It was in a bungalow belonging to a Sunset Strip hotel that comedy hero John Belushi died of a drugs overdose in March 1982.

- The Cajun Bistro at 8301 Sunset Strip was used in the final scenes of the Woody Allen film *Annie Hall*.

- The Viper Room, a nightclub owned by hunk Johnny Depp, was the scene of real-life Halloween horror on 31 October 1993, when actor River Phoenix collapsed and died in the doorway after taking drugs.

- During the 1940s, the Viper Room was called the Melody Room and was notorious as an illegal gambling den attracting clientele like Bugsy Siegel.

- Rock star Bruce Springsteen began his career at The Roxy at 9009 Sunset Strip.

- House of Blues at 8430 Sunset Strip is owned by Dan Aykroyd, who starred in the cult film *The Blues Brothers* with John Belushi.

- Comics including Richard Pryor and Jay Leno made their names at the Comedy Store at 8433 Sunset Strip.

- Stars who shop at celebrity cobblers Kenneth Cole Shoes at 8752 Sunset Strip have left their bare footprints in the cement outside the store – among them Elizabeth Taylor and Richard Gere.

- Marilyn Monroe had her first date with baseball legend Joe DiMaggio at the Villa Nova restaurant, at 9015 Sunset Strip (now known as the Rainbow Bar & Grill).

PAINE'S PAIN

Although Tom Paine is remembered as the heroic writer and thinker who coined the phrase 'United States', few admirers are aware of the trials and tribulations that his helpless corpse endured. Upon his death in 1809, he was buried in New Rochelle, New York State. But a decade later, ardent admirer William Cobbett exhumed the body and smuggled it to England, where he hoped it would be a rallying point for revolutionaries. In fact, Paine was widely hated in Britain and Cobbett quickly realised he could not risk depositing the body in a memorial as planned. Instead, he hawked the bones around the countryside as a curiosity and sold locks of Paine's hair. Cobbett died in 1835, leaving his son to care for the unburied Paine. It seems the remains were interred soon after, but not before some body parts had been severed and sold. It is thought that the brain stem was mummified by a sympathiser; the skull was kept in private ownership for years in an inscribed leather pouch, finally coming to public auction in Australia in 1988; a rib is believed to be in France; and there's a rumour that other bones were turned into buttons.

FIRST FLIGHT

The first commercial airline in the United States flew from Tampa to St Petersburg, Florida, in 1914.

BRITISH INFLUENCE

Eight of the first nine American presidents were born British subjects: Washington, John Adams, Jefferson, Madison, Monroe, John Quincy Adams, Jackson and Harrison. Van Buren was the first president born as a US citizen.

I DO, I DO

Andrew Jackson was the only president to marry the same woman twice. He married Mrs Rachel Robards, believing her to be properly divorced from her husband, but this turned out not to be the case. Two years later, when the divorce was completed, Jackson married her again.

BAT CAVE

Tens of thousands of bats live in the Carlsbad Caverns, New Mexico. The largest chamber of the Carlsbad Caverns is more than 10 football fields long and about 22 storeys high.

LAST RESTING PLACE

Washington Square is now one of Philadelphia's most prestigious addresses. Yet for nearly a century it was a cemetery, home to the bones of strangers to the city, before becoming a mass burial site for soldier victims of the Revolutionary War. With the colonial British operating a harsh regime at the nearby Walnut Street Jail, there were plenty more casualties bound for beneath the Square. When the Americans were victorious in their fight for Philly, it was British bodies that were destined to lie under the turf. Soon afterwards an epidemic of yellow fever sent still more to the grave, as about one in ten city residents perished. Only in 1825, when the square was finally named for America's first president, was it gentrified. In 1954, when the city fathers decided to honour an unknown soldier at a site in the square, archaeologists dug up several bodies before identifying one that probably belonged to a soldier. Even then they were unable to say for sure whether the bones belonged to one of Washington's finest or to a redcoat that fought against him.

MELUNGEONS

In remote corners of America, specifically the Appalachian Mountains, there reside the melungeons, members of an obscure race. In general terms, they are described as white folks with black skin, although their physical attributes are tremendously varied. Although scientific investigations are taking place and cultural comparisons have been made, no one really knows the origin of the melungeons. Some of the theories as to their background make astonishing reading:

• They are descendants of Spanish and Portuguese settlers who were long ago driven out of their communities.

• They come from the Gypsy or Rom fraternity. Gypsies were persecuted in England and may have been transported overseas in a form of ethnic cleansing.

• They were Turkish Muslims taken to America by the Spanish.

• Abandoned settlers from Elizabethan England mixed with American Indians and (later) African Americans, to form the melungeon community.

• They were Turkish slaves landed on Roanoke Island by Sir Francis Drake in 1586.

• They descend from the lost settlers of Roanoke, deposited there by an English expedition in 1587, but gone by 1590 (when a relief ship arrived).

HURRICANE HELL

The worst natural disaster in United States history was a hurricane that hit Galveston in 1900. More than 8,000 deaths were recorded.

TEXAS STARS

More species of bats live in Texas than in any other part of the United States.

AMERICA'S FAVOURITE CONSPIRACY THEORIES

John Wilkes Booth

- President Lincoln's assassin survived a shootout at a barn in Bowling Green, Virginia, where another man died with Booth's diary in his pocket. Booth then adopted various false names, fathered a child and subsequently committed suicide in 1903.

JFK

- He was not killed in Dallas but lives as a human vegetable on a remote isle.

- Lee Harvey Oswald was not the assassin.

- Kennedy was killed on the orders of the CIA or the Mob.

Marilyn Monroe

- She did not commit suicide, but was murdered by Robert Kennedy to prevent her from revealing embarrassing details of their affair.

- She was killed on the orders of the CIA or the Mob.

Elvis

- He did not die of a heart attack but survived and resides at his Graceland home, and can be seen peering out of windows at fans mourning by his supposed grave.

Apollo 11

- The Moon landing never took place and film footage was taken on a studio set.

9/11

- It was staged by the Israeli intelligence service Mossad.

- Explosives had already been planted in the Twin Towers.

- It was a military rather than a terrorist operation.

- The Pentagon was not hit by a plane at all but by something much smaller.

ALASKA – A NATURAL MARVEL

Nearly a third of Alaska lies within the Arctic Circle. It is so large that if a scale map of Alaska were to be superimposed on a map of the 48 lower states, Alaska would extend from coast to coast. Of the 20 highest peaks in the US, 17 are in Alaska, including Mount McKinley – which, at 6,194m (20,320ft), is the highest point in North America. Its capital city, Juneau, is the only one in the US that is accessible only by boat or plane.

INSIGHTS AND INSULTS

A book written for GIs in France in 1944 explaining some of the idiosyncrasies of the French became a belated bestseller in France in 2003, at a time when transatlantic relations were at an all-time low. Originally called *112 Gripes About The French*, it was reissued to mark the 50th anniversary of D-Day and highlights some of the most virulent complaints against the nation. Each is followed by a response, sometimes reinforcing the criticism and sometimes defending the French. No one knows the identity of the author – although he was surely from the US – but his wisdom has Gallic readers engrossed.

Complaint no. 7 offers food for thought on both sides of the Atlantic, given the accusation (levied by Americans against the French, following their refusal to join hostilities in Iraq) of being 'cheese-eating surrender monkeys'. 'We cannot trust the French' is the accusation penned during World War II. The answer given goes like this:

> 'It depends on what you mean by 'trust'. If you expect the French to react like Americans, you will be surely disappointed. They are not Americans. They are French. If you hope they will get a move on with things like us, you will also be disappointed. The French never get a move on. But in that they are like most of the world outside America.'

Complaint no. 34 asks: 'What have these blasted frog's leg eaters ever done for the world?' The answer is in the form of a list of French scientists and philosophers, artists and artisans.

Complaint no. 42 says: 'Their toilets are appalling.' 'True' is the given reply.

Sales leaped up when French–American relations deteriorated, partly through a French desire to better understand the American mentality.

(Source: *Daily Telegraph*, 25 July 03)

STILL WATERS

The Great Salt Lake, Utah, covers 5,440 square km (2,100 square miles) and has an average depth of 4m (13ft). The deepest point is 10.4m (34ft).

WINDY CITY

The highest wind speed recorded at ground level was at Mount Washington, New Hampshire, on 12 April 1934. The winds were three times faster than those in most hurricanes.

WHITE FLIGHT

Every spring, nearly 10,000 white pelicans with a wingspan of 2.7m (9ft) migrate from the Gulf of Mexico to Medicine Lake in northeastern Montana.

STARTLING ROCK

Nebraska's Chimney Rock was the most often mentioned landmark in journal entries by travellers on the Oregon Trail.

DESERT RAT

In Death Valley, Nevada, the kangaroo rat can live its entire life without drinking a drop of liquid.

PEAKS AND TROUGHS

California contains the highest and the lowest points in continental USA within 160km (100 miles) of one another. Mount Whitney is 4,418m (14,495ft) high while Bad Water in Death Valley is 86m (282ft) below sea level.

TALL TREES

Sequoia National Park is home to the largest living tree, with a trunk that measures 31m (102ft) in circumference. Some of the giant redwoods in the park are more than 2,000 years old. In 1925, a giant sequoia in Kings Canyon National Park was designated to be the national Christmas tree. It is now over 90m (300ft) tall.

BOLT MENACE

Clearwater, Florida, has the highest rate of lightning strikes per capita of any city in the United States.

LONE EAGLE

In May 1927, Captain Charles Lindbergh won the race to complete the first solo, nonstop transatlantic flight when his aircraft, a Ryan NYP monoplane called *Spirit Of St Louis* touched down at Le Bourget airport in France. The 5,750km (3,600 mile) crossing took 33 hours and 39 minutes to complete.

Lindbergh was one of numerous contenders for a $25,000 (£15,500) prize on offer for the first nonstop flight between New York and Paris. More than 100,000 people were waiting to greet him at the French airport after his triumph. He had flown at heights varying between 3m (10ft) and 300m (1,000ft) at an average speed of 172km (107.5 miles) per hour, staying awake by eating home-made sandwiches. Emerging as a national hero, he became known as 'The Lone Eagle', and the following year President Coolidge awarded him the Congressional Medal of Honor. He was so popular that a dance, the Lindy Hop, was named for him.

Fame and fortune failed to bring him happiness, however. On 2 March 1932 his baby son, also called Charles, was kidnapped from the family home in New Jersey, sparking a massive manhunt. Two months later the bludgeoned body of the 20-month-old boy was found in woodland 8km (5 miles) from the Lindbergh mansion. Bruno Hauptmann was executed on 3 April 1936 after being found guilty of kidnapping and murdering the infant. Lindbergh later vexed public opinion by expressing support for Hitler's regime prior to America's entry into World War II.

COMIC CAPER

Metropolis, the home town of Superman, really exists – in southern Illinois.

SHE'S A DOLL

The original Barbie is from Willows, Wisconsin. Her full name is Barbie Millicent Roberts. Today there are more than 200 different types of Barbie.

HIDEBOUND

It takes 3,000 cows to supply the NFL with enough leather for a year's supply of footballs.

CLASS WAR

In March 1925 it became illegal to explain the theory of evolution to schoolchildren in Tennessee. According to state governor Austin Peay, who signed the Butler Act into law, it was a 'distinct protest against an irreligious tendency to exalt so-called science and deny the Bible'. A new textbook avoiding all mention of evolution was issued to children in the state. Tennessee was the first of six states to take action on the thorny issue of man's evolution from the apes.

Peay went on to pronounce that 'The very integrity of the Bible in its statement of man's divine creation is denied by any theory that man descended or has ascended from any lower order of animals.' By May, the first trial of a teacher (John Scopes of Dayton) accused of spreading the evolutionary word had begun. Two months later he was found guilty and fined $100 (£62). Soon afterwards, the court's decision and the Butler Act itself were overturned. The court case was brought to the screen in *Inherit The Wind*, starring Spencer Tracey and Frederic Marsh. Even today, it is re-enacted by way of a festival, sponsored by those with a scientific bent.

PATRIOTIC PLACE

America's national anthem was written by Francis Scott Key, a Maryland lawyer. It is believed he wrote it on 14 September 1818, while watching the bombardment of Fort McHenry in Baltimore Harbour. Since 30 May 1949, the United States flag has flown continuously over the monument, marking the site of his birthplace at Terra Rubra Farm, Carroll County, Keymar, Maryland.

BIG BUY

In 1803, the United States paid France $15 million (£9 million) for the Louisiana Territory, 2.1 million square km (828,000 square miles) of land west of the Mississippi River. The lands acquired in what has become known as the Louisiana Purchase stretched from the Mississippi River to the Rocky Mountains and from the Gulf of Mexico to the Canadian border. Thirteen states were carved from the Louisiana Territory, and the purchase nearly doubled the size of the United States.

CONFLICT VICTIMS

In the War of 1812 – between the US and Great Britain – more than half of all Americans killed in action came from Kentucky.

US PRESIDENTS

1. George Washington (1789)
2. John Adams (1797)
3. Thomas Jefferson (1801)
4. James Madison (1809)
5. James Monroe (1817)
6. John Quincy Adams (1825)
7. Andrew Jackson (1829)
8. Martin Van Buren (1837)
9. William Henry Harrison (1841)
10. John Tyler (1841)
11. James Knox Polk (1845)
12. Zachary Taylor (1849)
13. Millard Fillmore (1850)
14. Franklin Pierce (1853)
15. James Buchanan (1857)
16. Abraham Lincoln (1861)
17. Andrew Johnson (1865)
18. Ulysses S Grant (1869)
19. Rutherford B Hayes (1877)
20. James A Garfield (1881)
21. Chester A Arthur (1881)
22. S Grover Cleveland (1885)
23. Benjamin Harrison (1889)
24. S Grover Cleveland (1893)
25. William McKinley (1897)
26. Theodore Roosevelt (1901)
27. William H Taft (1909)
28. T Woodrow Wilson (1913)
29. Warren G Harding (1921)
30. Calvin Coolidge (1923)
31. Herbert Hoover (1929)
32. Franklin Delano Roosevelt (1933)
33. Harry S Truman (1945)
34. Dwight D Eisenhower (1953)
35. John F Kennedy (1961)

36. Lyndon Baines Johnson (1963)
37. Richard Milhous Nixon (1969)
38. Gerald R Ford (1974)
39. James (Jimmy) Earl Carter (1977)
40. Ronald W Reagan (1981)
41. George Herbert Walker Bush (1989)
42. William Jefferson Clinton (1992)
43. George Walker Bush (2000)

WOMEN COUNT

According to the 2000 census, the overall percentage of 'female persons' in the USA was 50.9. The lowest number of women were found in Alaska, where they made up 48.3 per cent of the population, and the highest was in the District of Columbia, where they made up 52.9 per cent.

CAMERA ACTION

It has been estimated that 5 per cent of all Kodak film made is used for taking pictures at Disney attractions.

DEAD CENTRE

The town of Rugby, North Dakota, is the geographical centre of continental North America. A rock obelisk about 4.5m (15ft) tall, flanked by poles flying the United States and Canadian flags, marks the location.

WHEELIE WHEELIE TRUE

The nation's only mobile national monuments are the St Charles streetcar line in New Orleans and the San Francisco cable cars.

FACE OF AMERICA

Fountain, Colorado, was chosen as the United States' millennium city. It was found by a Queens College sociologist to represent most accurately, within one city, the population make-up of the United States.

US GEM

The Montana Yogo Sapphire is the only North American gem to be included in England's Crown Jewels.

US STATES IN THE ORDER THEY ENTERED THE UNION (EXCLUDING THE ORIGINAL 13 STATES)

Vermont	4 March 1791
Kentucky	1 June 1792
Tennessee	1 June 1796
Ohio	1 March 1803
Louisiana	30 April 1812
Indiana	11 December 1816
Mississippi	10 December 1817
Illinois	3 December 1818
Alabama	14 December 1819
Maine	15 March 1820
Missouri	10 August 1821
Arkansas	15 June 1836
Michigan	26 January 1837
Florida	3 March 1845
Texas	29 December 1845
Iowa	28 December 1846
Wisconsin	29 May 1848
California	9 September 1850
Minnesota	11 May 1858
Oregon	14 February 1859
Kansas	29 January 1861
West Virginia	20 June 1863
Nevada	31 October 1864
Nebraska	1 March 1867
Colorado	1 August 1876
North Dakota	2 November 1889
South Dakota	2 November 1889
Montana	8 November 1889
Washington	11 November 1889
Idaho	3 July 1890
Wyoming	10 July 1890
Utah	4 January 1896
Oklahoma	16 November 1907
New Mexico	6 January 1912
Arizona	14 February 1912
Alaska	3 January 1959
Hawaii	21 August 1959

ROAD SAFETY

In Hartford, Connecticut, under no circumstances may you cross the road walking on your hands.

LIBERACE TRIBUTE

Nevada is the only state with an entire museum devoted to the life and times of entertainer Liberace.

MISERABLE MIDAS

Howard Hughes was born to a rich family and his Midas touch led him to increase his personal wealth many times over. He also established the land-plane speed record in 1935, built a massive wooden plane capable of carrying 750 passengers, and launched Jean Harlow, Paul Muni and Jane Russell as stars of the silver screen. Yet it is for none of these feats that he is remembered.

On hearing his name, most people recall Howard Hughes as a bizarre recluse, scuttling secretively between luxury hotels in an extraordinary attempt to protect his privacy. He grew emaciated from a diet of fad foods and prescription drugs, and inhabited a largely twilight world as he watched favourite movies obsessively day and night. At the time of his death in 1976, he had long grey hair, uncut fingernails and had lived behind closed doors for a quarter of a century. His fortune was worth an estimated £1 billion ($1.5 billion).

REMORSELESS MORSE

The longest Morse code telegram ever sent was the Nevada State constitution, sent from Carson City to Washington, DC in 1864. The transmission must have taken several hours.

BLITZ BLUNDER

Boise City, Oklahoma, was the only city in the United States to be bombed during World War II. On the night of Monday 5 July 1943, at approximately 12:30am, a B-17 bomber based at Dalhart Army Air Base – 80km (50 miles) to the south of Boise City – dropped six practice bombs on the sleeping town.

TWO-SIDED

Oregon's state flag pictures a beaver on its reverse side. It is the only state flag to carry two separate designs.

CLAIM TO FAME

Although there's no evidence to prove it, Betsy Ross reputedly stitched the first American flag in Philadelphia.

CLEARANCE, CLARENCE

Actor Jimmy Stewart was born and raised in the town of Indiana, Pennsylvania. Each year at Christmas the downtown area is decorated in the theme of arguably his most famous film, *It's A Wonderful Life*.

ONE OUT OF EVERY EIGHT...

...United States residents live in California.

POLITICAL QUOTES

'I am waging a war in this campaign...against the four Horsemen of the present Republican leadership: The Horsemen of Destruction, Delay, Deceit and Despair.'
Franklin Roosevelt in the year he was elected president

'We're eyeball to eyeball and the other fellow just blinked.'
Dean Rusk, US Secretary of State, on the Cuban crisis of 1962

'Ich bin ein Berliner.'
President **John F Kennedy** speaking in 1963 to Germans in West Berlin, left isolated when the communist Iron Curtain came down in Europe (meaning all free men stood shoulder-to-shoulder with Berliners)

'I have a dream that the sons of former slaves and the sons of former slave owners would sit together at the table of brotherhood.'
Martin Luther King, at a civil rights demonstration in 1963

'Join me and march along the road...that leads to the Great Society, where no child will go unfed...where every human being has dignity and every worker has a job.'
Lyndon Johnson, campaigning for presidency in 1964

'I ain't got no quarrel with them Viet Congs.'
Muhammad Ali when he was stripped of his world heavyweight title
following his refusal to join the US Army

'This is the greatest week in the history of the world since the Creation.'
Richard Nixon to the returned astronauts who made the first lunar landing
in 1969

'You ain't seen nothing yet.'
Ronald Reagan, on his re-election in November 1984

'You can no more win a war than you can win an earthquake.'
Jeanette Rankin, first woman elected to the US House of Representatives,
speaking after the attack on Pearl Harbour in 1941

'Speak softly and carry a big stick.'
Theodore Roosevelt on foreign policy

'The business of America is business.'
Calvin Coolidge in 1925, shortly before the Great Depression

'You may fool all the people some of the time; you can even fool some of
the people all the time; but you can't fool all of the people all the time.'
Abraham Lincoln

'Give me liberty or give me death.'
Attributed to **Patrick Henry** at Richmond's St John's Church

BLOOMING GREAT

An early form of anaesthesia using ethylene gas was discovered in 1908.
Carnation growers in Chicago asked a pair of botanists to find out why
their flowers wouldn't bloom, and the culprit was found to be the ethylene
used to light the greenhouses. Concerns over its potentially harmful effect
on animals and humans led to tests, though these discovered that (far from
being harmful) it actually had anaesthetic effects.

GALE FORCE

The world's largest wind generator is on the island of Oahu. The windmill
has two 122m- (400ft-) long blades fixed on the top of a tower that stands
twenty storeys high.

TAN MAN

Benjamin Green, a pharmacist from Miami Beach, Florida, invented the very first suntan cream in 1944. He apparently achieved this by cooking cocoa butter in a granite pot on his wife's stove – though no one mentions why he didn't use his own.

MASSACRE AT WOUNDED KNEE

Rising in southwest South Dakota and flowing northwest to the White River, Wounded Knee Creek is the site of the last major battle of the Indian wars. After the death of Sitting Bull, a band of Sioux led by Big Foot fled into the badlands, where they were captured by the Seventh Cavalry on 28 December 1890 and brought to the creek. The next day, the Sioux were supposedly disarmed, but when a medicine man threw dust into the air a warrior pulled a gun and wounded an officer. The US troops opened fire, and within minutes almost 200 men, women and children were shot. The soldiers later claimed that it was difficult to distinguish the Sioux women from the men.

LAST GASPS

George Appel, gangster:
'Well, gentlemen, you about to see a baked Appel.'
(Said to reporters before he met his death in the electric chair in 1928.)

Phineas Taylor Barnum, showman:
'How were the receipts in Madison Square Garden?'

Leonard Bernstein, composer, pianist and conductor:
'What's this?'

Billy the Kid (William Bonney), gunman:
'Who is it?'

John Wilkes Booth, assassin of President Lincoln:
'Tell mother, tell mother, I died for my country…useless…useless…'

Lenny Bruce, comedian:
'Do you know where I can get any shit?'

James Buchanan, 15th US president:
'Whatever the result may be, I shall carry to my grave the consciousness that at least I meant well for my country.'

Luther Burbank, horticulturalist:
'I don't feel good.'

Kit Carson, American frontiersman:
'Wish I had time for just one more bowl of chili.'

Stephen Grover Cleveland, 22nd and 24th US president:
'I have tried so hard to do right.'

Hart Crane, poet:
'Goodbye, everybody.'
(While on board a steamship returning from Mexico, Crane bid his fellow passengers farewell and jumped overboard.)

Bing Crosby, actor:
'It was a great game.'
(He keeled over on a golf course in Spain.)

Isadora Duncan, dancer:
'Adieu mes amis. Je vais à la gloire!'
('Goodbye, my friends. I'm going for glory.' Said to friends before she set off for a drive in a red Bugatti sports car in the south of France. Unknown to her, the fringe of her shawl was draped close to the rear wheel, and at its first rotation the garment got snarled up and broke her neck.)

George Eastman, founder of the Eastman Kodak empire:
'My work is done, why wait?'

Thomas A Edison, inventor:
'It's very beautiful over there.'

Douglas Fairbanks Sr, swashbuckler:
'Never felt better.'

WC Fields, comedian:
'God damn the whole friggin' world and everyone in it but you, Carlotta.'

Sean Flannagan, to his executioner in New York in 1989:
'I love you.'

James French, murderer:
'How about this for a headline in tomorrow's paper: French fries.'
(He met his death in the electric chair in Oklahoma in 1966.)

Johnny Frank Garrett, murderer:
'I'd like to thank my family for loving me and taking care of me. And the rest of the world can kiss my ass.'
(Garrett brutally murdered a Catholic nun in 1981. Caught, tried and

LAST GASPS (CONT'D)

convicted, he was finally executed in 1991, after exhausting his legal appeals process.)

Gary Gilmore, murderer:
'Let's do it.'

Alexander Hamilton, one of America's Founding Fathers:
'This is a mortal wound, doctor.'

O Henry (William Sidney Porter):
'Don't turn down the light. I'm afraid to go home in the dark.'
(O Henry was Porter's pen name, an American writer famous for his short stories – especially the Christmas favourite, 'The Gift Of The Magi'. His last words were part of a song that was popular at the time of his death.)

Conrad N Hilton, hotelier:
'Leave the shower curtain on the inside of the tub.'
(Hilton was born in San Antonio, New Mexico, and began his career by renting out rooms. On his deathbed, he was asked if he had any last words of wisdom for the world.)

Al Jolson, entertainer:
'This is it! I'm going. I'm going.'

Wilson Mizner, writer and gambler:
'Why should I talk to you? I've just been talking to your boss.'
(On his deathbed, he briefly regained consciousness before dying, and found a priest standing over him. Mizner waved the priest away, uttering these words.)

Eugene O'Neill, Nobel and Pulitzer prize-winning dramatist:
'Born in a hotel room – and God damn it – died in a hotel room.'

Franklin Roosevelt, 32nd president:
'I have a terrific headache.'

'Uncle John' Sedgwick, commander in the Army of the Potomac during the Civil War:
'They couldn't hit an elephant at this dist—.'
(His officers and men urged him to take cover from small arms fire, but Sedgwick scoffed at their concerns, 'What! What men! This will never do, dodging from single bullets!' As the general spoke his last words, he was shot in the head by an enemy sniper.)

COPY THAT

The Anne Hathaway Cottage at Wessington Springs is the only structure in the US Midwest to feature a thatched roof. The cottage is styled after the original Hathaway home in Stratford-upon-Avon, England. Anne Hathaway was William Shakespeare's wife.

SMALL CONGREGATION

Oneida, New York, contains the world's smallest church – with dimensions of 1.1m by 1.8m (3¹/₂ft by 6ft).

BIG BUG

The world's largest model bug is on the roof of New England Pest Control in Providence, Rhode Island. It's a big blue termite, 17.7m (58ft) long, and (fortunately) 928 times actual termite size.

CHEERS

Built in 1873, the White Horse Tavern, Rhode Island, is the oldest operating tavern in the United States.

RITE ON

New England's oldest Masonic temple in Warren, Rhode Island, was built in the 18th century with timbers from British frigates sunk in Newport Harbour during the Revolutionary War (1775–83).

BALL WALL

The walls of the American fort on Sullivan Island, in Charleston Harbour, were made of spongy palmetto logs. This proved helpful in protecting the fort because the British cannonballs bounced off the defences.

A ROUTE 66 BOUQUET

Route 66 runs for 4,067km (2,542 miles) from Chicago to Los Angeles. A bouquet made from the state flowers of all the states it crosses would consist of: native violet (Illinois), hawthorn (Missouri), sunflower (Kansas), mistletoe (Oklahoma), blue bonnet (Texas), yucca (New Mexico), saguaro cactus (Arizona) and golden poppy (California).

AROUND THE WORLD IN DISNEY-SPEAK

Mickey Mouse

Arabic	Mickey
Czech	Mickey Mouse
Danish	Mickey Mouse
English	Mickey Mouse
French	Mickey
German	Micky Maus
Greek	Mikki Maous
Icelandic	Mikki Mús
Indonesian	Miki Tikus
Italian	Topolino
Russian	Mikki Maus
Spanish	El Ratón Mickey/Mickey Mouse

Donald Duck

Arabic	Battouta
Czech	Kacer Donald
Danish	Anders And
English	Donald Duck
French	Donald Duck
German	Donald Duck/Schnatterich
Greek	Ntonalt Ntak
Icelandic	Andrés Önd
Indonesian	Donal Bebek
Italian	Paolino/Paperino
Russian	Donald Dak
Spanish	El Pato Donald

Huey, Dewey and Louie – Donald's Nephews

Arabic	Sou Sou, Tou Tou, Fou Fou
Czech	Bubíkem, Dulíkem a Kulíkem
Danish	Rip, Rap og Rup
English	Huey, Dewey and Louie
French	Loulou, Riri et Fifi
German	Tick, Trick und Track
Greek	Hiui, Ntiui, Liui
Icelandic	Malli, Palli, Kalli
Indonesian	Kwik, Kwek dan Kwak
Italian	Qui, Quo, Qua
Russian	Billy, Willy, Dilly
Spanish	Jorgito, Juanito y Jaimito

Uncle Scrooge – Donald's billionaire uncle

Arabic	Amm Da Hab
Czech	Strycek Skrblík
Danish	Onkel Joakim/Joakim von And
English	Uncle Scrooge/Scrooge McDuck
French	Oncle Picsou/Oncle Harpagon/Balthazar Picsou
German	Onkel Dagobert/Dagobert Duck
Greek	Thios Skroutz/Skroutz MakNtak
Icelandic	Jóakim Önd
Indonesian	Paman Gober/Gober Bebek
Italian	Zio Paperone/Paperon de Paperoni
Russian	Djdj Skrudg/Skrudg MakDak
Spanish	Tío Gilito/Gil Pato

Goofy

Arabic	Bondock
Czech	Goofy
Danish	Fedtmule
English	Goofy
French	Dingo/Goufy
German	Goofy
Greek	Gkoufi
Icelandic	Ferdinand
Indonesian	Gufi
Italian	Pippo
Russian	Gufi
Spanish	Goofy

CHEW ON THAT!

In Louisiana, biting someone with your natural teeth is considered a simple assault, but to bite someone with your false teeth is considered an aggravated assault.

BAT CAVE

The most crowded mammal homes are the caves used by female free-tailed bats in Texas. In one of these caves, 10 million females gave birth (one baby each) over the course of ten days.

HIGH-PROFILE TITANIC VICTIMS

Isidor Straus – co-owner of Macy's department store

John Jacob Astor – one of the world's wealthiest men, returning from honeymoon

Major Archibald Butt – military aide to President William Taft

Benjamin Guggenheim – millionaire

Thomas Andrews – managing director of shipbuilders Harland and Wolff

Colonel John Weir – mine owner and benefactor

Charles M Hays – president of the Grand Trunk Railway

Jacques Futrelle – author

William Thomas Stead – journalist and author

Henry B Harris – theatre impresario

Washington A Roebling III – grandson of the Brooklyn Bridge designer and steel company president

LARGEST WINNING MARGINS IN THE SUPER BOWL

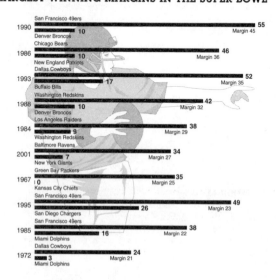

San Francisco 49ers
1990 — 55
10
Denver Broncos — Margin 45

Chicago Bears
1986 — 46
10
New England Patriots — Margin 36

Dallas Cowboys
1993 — 52
17
Buffalo Bills — Margin 35

Washington Redskins
1988 — 42
10
Denver Broncos — Margin 32

Los Angeles Raiders
1984 — 38
9
Washington Redskins — Margin 29

Baltimore Ravens
2001 — 34
7
New York Giants — Margin 27

Green Bay Packers
1967 — 35
0
Kansas City Chiefs — Margin 25

San Francisco 49ers
1995 — 49
26
San Diego Chargers — Margin 23

San Francisco 49ers
1985 — 38
16
Miami Dolphins — Margin 22

Dallas Cowboys
1972 — 24
3
Miami Dolphins — Margin 21

BAKED RACCOON

This is a Native American recipe, as posted on the web by Joy Downing:

Ingredients
- 1 raccoon
- salt and pepper
- onion
- garlic cloves
- carrots
- potatoes
- tomato juice

Note: You can put in your favourite leaf spice.

Preparation
1. Clean raccoon; remove all fat; cut up.

2. Put in large pot with water to cover raccoon; add salt.

3. Bring to boil and simmer until tender.

4. Remove meat from pan and put in baking dish.

5. Add onion, carrots; cut up potatoes; salt and pepper to taste

6. Pour tomato juice over top of every thing; then cover.

7. Bake at 180°C (350°F/Gas mark 4) for 1 hour or until veggies are done.

Serves 3 to 4.

BROKEN DREAMS, TRAMPLED TERRITORY

Despite having been set aside 'for eternity' as Indian territory, Oklahoma was opened up for white settlement in 1889. Between noon and sundown on 22 April, more than 10,000 people flocked in to claim the new lands, making Oklahoma City the biggest boom town of the 1889 land rush.

LIGHTING UP THEIR LIVES

After hitting the big time, tap dancer and actor Bill Robinson (1878–1949) – better known as Mr Bojangles – donated a traffic light to a busy junction in his old neighbourhood in Richmond, Virginia, so local children could cross the street in safety.

INDY CAR CHAMPIONS 1909 –2003

1909 George Robertson	1910 Ray Harroun
1911 Ralph Mulford	1912 Ralph DeParma
1913 Earl Cooper	1914 Ralph DeParma
1915 Earl Cooper	1916 Dario Resta
1917 Earl Cooper	1918 Ralph Mulford
1919 Howard Wilcox	1920 Tommy Milton
1921 Tommy Milton	1922 Jimmy Murphy
1923 Eddie Hearne	1924 Jimmy Murphy
1925 Peter DePaolo	1926 Harry Hartz
1927 Peter DePaolo	1928 Louie Meyer
1929 Louie Meyer	1930 Billy Arnold
1931 Louis Schneider	1932 Bob Carey
1933 Louie Meyer	1934 Bill Cummings
1935 Kelly Petillo	1936 Mauri Rose
1937 Wilbur Shaw	1938 Floyd Roberts
1939 Wilbur Shaw	1940 Rex Mays
1941 Rex Mays	1942–5 No racing
1946 Ted Horn	1947 Ted Horn
1948 Ted Horn	1949 Johnny Parsons
1950 Henry Banks	1951 Tony Bettenhausen Sr
1952 Chuck Stevenson	1953 Sam Hanks
1954 Jimmy Bryan	1955 Bob Swikert
1956 Jimmy Bryan	1957 Jimmy Bryan
1958 Tony Bettenhausen Sr	1959 Rodger Ward
1960 AJ Foyt	1961 AJ Foyt
1962 Rodger Ward	1963 AJ Foyt
1964 AJ Foyt	1965 Mario Andretti
1966 Mario Andretti	1967 AJ Foyt
1968 Bobby Unser	1969 Mario Andretti
1970 Al Unser	1971 Joe Leonard
1972 Joe Leonard	1973 Roger McCluskey
1974 Bobby Unser	1975 AJ Foyt
1976 Gordon Johncock	1977 Tom Sneva
1978 Tom Sneva	1979 AJ Foyt (USAC)/Rick Mears (CART)
1980 Johnny Rutherford	1981 Rick Mears
1982 Rick Mears	1983 Al Unser
1984 Mario Andretti	1985 Al Unser
1986 Bobby Rahal	1987 Bobby Rahal
1988 Danny Sullivan	1989 Emerson Fittipaldi
1990 Al Unser Jr	1991 Michael Andretti

1992 Bobby Rahal	1993 Nigel Mansell
1994 Al Unser Jr	1995 Jacques Villeneuve
1996 Jimmy Vasser	1997 Alex Zanardi
1998 Alex Zanardi	1999 Pablo Montoya
2000 Gil de Ferran	2001 Gil de Ferran
2002 Cristiano da Matta	2003 Paul Tracy

AMERICAN LITERARY GIANTS

William Burroughs (1914–97)

Born in St Louis, Missouri, Burroughs became synonymous with the Beat movement that included poet Allen Ginsberg and writer Jack Kerouac. Burroughs' book *The Naked Lunch* is regarded as his masterpiece and the template for the rest of his literary output. Employing the 'stream of consciousness' style, *The Naked Lunch* is a nightmarish scenario of underworld figures, lunatics and secret agents against a backdrop of sadomasochism and diabolism. Burroughs shared with Ginsberg and Kerouac an abiding affection for alcohol, drugs and junk food. He married a fellow drug addict called Joan Vollmer, whom he accidentally shot and killed in 1951. Ironically this tragedy was to mark Burroughs' birth as a writer. He himself wrote, 'I am forced to the appalling conclusion that I would never have become a writer but for Joan's death.'

Raymond Chandler (1888–1959)

Chandler created a hard-boiled world of detectives for his enduring character Philip Marlowe, who was introduced in his first novel, *The Big Sleep* (1939). He worked as a scriptwriter in Hollywood in the 1940s and worked most notably on Alfred Hitchcock's *Strangers On A Train*. A serial womaniser, drinker and manic depressive, he ended his years as a semi-recluse.

William Faulkner (1897–1962)

Faulkner was another writer who engaged in experimental literary styles in novels like *Absalom, Absalom* and *Light In August*. He wrote scripts for Hollywood including *The Big Sleep*, won the Nobel prize for literature in 1949 and two subsequent Pulitzer prizes. In his final years, he took up drinking copious amounts and died after falling off his horse.

F Scott Fitzgerald (1896–1940)

Born as Francis Scott Key Fitzgerald, he later abridged his name to get it on the front cover of his books. Fitzgerald was renowned for living life in the fast lane, where he died at the tender age of 44, leaving behind a trail of personal destruction and a place in the pantheon of American literati with *The Great Gatsby* and *Tender Is The Night*. Depression and alcoholism dogged his final years.

AMERICAN LITERARY GIANTS (CONT'D)

Joseph Heller (1923–99)

Critically acclaimed US novelist, principally for his first published novel *Catch-22*. A famous quote from the novel went thus: 'Some men are born mediocre, some men achieve mediocrity, and some men have mediocrity thrust upon them.' Heller collaborated on *Casino Royale*, the spoof James Bond movie. He died in 1999, following a heart attack.

Ernest Hemingway (1899–1961)

Short-story writer and novelist identified by his adventurous plots contained within a spartan, yet visually demonstrative writing style that led to much of his work being transferred to Hollywood and the big screen. He was nominated for the Pulitzer prize in 1941, for his novel *For Whom The Bell Tolls*, but this was subsequently vetoed by right-wing members of the prize committee, whose politics were at odds with his own. He nevertheless won the Nobel prize for literature 14 years later. His tempestuous life bore all the hallmarks of the characters in his books, particularly bullfighters and big-game hunters. He volunteered as an ambulance driver in the Spanish Civil War, married four times and ended his days in alcohol-fuelled oblivion before taking his own life. With an oeuvre of books that include *The Old Man And The Sea* and *A Farewell To Arms*, Hemingway occupies a lofty position in the temple of literature.

Jack Kerouac (1922–69)

Born Jean-Louis Lebris de Kerouac, he was another bell-ringer for the Beat Generation. His most famous work, *On The Road*, took eight years to write and was produced on a scroll of paper over 30m (100ft) long. It found great favour with the American public, but less so with fellow author Truman Capote, who said, 'That's not writing. That's just typing.' Still, Keroauc became an influential role model for those attracted to the bohemian lifestyle. He died as a result of his indulgent lifestyle, obese and housebound.

Edgar Allan Poe (1809–49)

Edgar Allan Poe's life was as bizarre as his fantastic tales. The date and place of his birth (and, indeed, his grave) are still matters of conjecture for many involved in documenting his life. What is certain is that Poe left a rich legacy of poetry and short stories, the like of which have influenced many, and have seen him introduce the detective into mainstream literature. Much has been written (and possibly invented) about his imbibing of alcohol and an equal propensity for drugs, although there is little evidence to support these claims. Poe did in fact use alcohol as a crook during his wife Virginia's long illness, which culminated in her death in 1847. He died five days after being found in a delirious state in a Baltimore street, having allegedly been set upon by muggers. His most famous works included *Tales Of The Grotesque And Arabesque* (which contains one of his most famous works, 'The Fall Of The House Of Usher'), *The Raven And Other Poems* and *The Pit And The Pendulum*.

JD Salinger (1919–)

Major US author who may or may not live as a recluse in New Hampshire. Equally famed for his retreat from public life as for his only published novel to date, *The Catcher In The Rye*, a coming-of-age tale that revolves around teenager Holden Caulfield.

John Steinbeck (1902–68)

Steinbeck's *The Grapes Of Wrath* won the Pulitzer prize and was made into a classic 1940s film that awakened America's social consciousness. Other important works included *Of Mice And Men* and *East Of Eden*. He was awarded the Nobel prize for literature in 1962.

Tennessee Williams (1911–83)

Unarguably America's most influential playwright, Williams wrote some of the 20th century's most enduring plays, including *The Glass Menagerie*, *Cat On A Hot Tin Roof*, *The Night Of The Iguana* and *A Streetcar Named Desire*. He collected Pulitzer prizes as a pastime and his works were immortalised on celluloid, notably in *Streetcar* (starring Vivien Leigh and Marlon Brando) and *Cat On A Hot Tin Roof* (with Burl Ives, Elizabeth Taylor and Paul Newman). A closet homosexual who finally outed himself in his memoirs, Williams's final years descended into a world of hypochondria, drink and drugs.

RATTLE AND SHAKE

A rattlesnake's rattle can be heard 30m (100ft) away.

ON AIR

On 18 January 1903, in the first transatlantic radio message ever transmitted, President Roosevelt sent greetings from the American people to residents of the British Empire. It was sent by Morse code from South Wellfleet, Massachusetts, and received at the Marconi radio station at Poldhu, Cornwall. Britain's King Edward VII replied from his home in Sandringham, Norfolk, the following day.

BEST ACTOR OSCARS

Date	Actor	Film
1928	Emil Jennings	*The Last Command/The Way Of All Flesh*
1929	Warner Baxter	*In Old Arizona*
1930	George Arliss	*Disraeli*
1931	Lionel Barrymore	*A Free Soul*
1932	Wallace Beery	*The Champ*
	Fredric March	*Dr Jekyll And Mr Hyde*
1933	Charles Laughton	*The Private Life of Henry VIII*
1934	Clark Gable	*It Happened One Night*
1935	Victor McLaglen	*The Informer*
1936	Paul Muni	*The Story Of Louis Pasteur*
1937	Spencer Tracy	*Captains Courageous*
1938	Spencer Tracy	*Boys Town*
1939	Robert Donat	*Goodbye Mr Chips*
1940	James Stewart	*The Philadelphia Story*
1941	Gary Cooper	*Sergeant York*
1942	James Cagney	*Yankee Doodle Dandy*
1943	Paul Lukas	*Watch On The Rhine*
1944	Bing Crosby	*Going My Way*
1945	Ray Milland	*The Lost Weekend*
1946	Fredric March	*The Best Years Of Our Lives*
1947	Ronald Colman	*A Double Life*
1948	Laurence Olivier	*Hamlet*
1949	Broderick Crawford	*All The King's Men*
1950	José Ferrer	*Cyrano De Bergerac*
1951	Humphrey Bogart	*The African Queen*
1952	Gary Cooper	*High Noon*
1953	William Holden	*Stalag 17*
1954	Marlon Brando	*On the Waterfront*
1955	Ernest Borgnine	*Marty*
1956	Yul Brynner	*The King And I*
1957	Alec Guinness	*The Bridge On The River Kwai*
1958	David Niven	*Separate Tables*
1959	Charlton Heston	*Ben Hur*
1960	Burt Lancaster	*Elmer Gantry*
1961	Maximillian Schell	*Judgment At Nuremberg*
1962	Gregory Peck	*To Kill A Mockingbird*
1963	Sidney Poitier	*Lilies Of The Field*
1964	Rex Harrison	*My Fair Lady*
1965	Lee Marvin	*Cat Ballou*

1966	Paul Scofield	*A Man For All Seasons*
1967	Rod Steiger	*In The Heat Of The Night*
1968	Cliff Robertson	*Charly*
1969	John Wayne	*True Grit*
1970	George C Scott	*Patton* (refused)
1971	Gene Hackman	*The French Connection*
1972	Marlon Brando	*The Godfather* (refused)
1973	Jack Lemmon	*Save The Tiger*
1974	Art Carney	*Harry And Tonto*
1975	Jack Nicholson	*One Flew Over The Cuckoo's Nest*
1976	Peter Finch	*Network*
1977	Richard Dreyfuss	*The Goodbye Girl*
1978	Jon Voight	*Coming Home*
1979	Dustin Hoffman	*Kramer vs Kramer*
1980	Robert De Niro	*Raging Bull*
1981	Henry Fonda	*On Golden Pond*
1982	Ben Kingsley	*Gandhi*
1983	Robert Duvall	*Tender Mercies*
1984	F Murray Abraham	*Amadeus*
1985	William Hurt	*Kiss Of The Spider Woman*
1986	Paul Newman	*The Color Of Money*
1987	Michael Douglas	*Wall Street*
1988	Dustin Hoffman	*Rain Man*
1989	Daniel Day Lewis	*My Left Foot*
1990	Jeremy Irons	*Reversal Of Fortune*
1991	Anthony Hopkins	*Silence Of The Lambs*
1992	Al Pacino	*Scent Of A Woman*
1993	Tom Hanks	*Philadelphia*
1994	Tom Hanks	*Forrest Gump*
1995	Nicolas Cage	*Leaving Las Vegas*
1996	Geoffrey Rush	*Shine*
1997	Jack Nicholson	*As Good As It Gets*
1998	Roberto Benigni	*Life Is Beautiful*
1999	Kevin Spacey	*American Beauty*
2000	Russell Crowe	*Gladiator*
2001	Denzel Washington	*Training Day*
2002	Adrien Brody	*The Pianist*

FAST TRACK

The roadrunner can fly, but it prefers to race along the ground in its desert home. Sprinting along, it has clocked up speeds of 26kph (16mph).

INEQUALITY OF THE SEXES

In Maryland in 1704, when colonial cultivation of the region got under way, there were just 7,000 women, while the male population exceeded 30,000.

BEFORE THEY WERE FAMOUS...

Elvis was a truck driver
Jimi Hendrix stacked supermarket shelves
Cary Grant was a lifeguard at Coney Island
Burt Lancaster was a trapeze artist
Clark Gable worked in a tyre factory
Sylvester Stallone was a lion cage cleaner
Danny DeVito was a hairdresser
Bette Midler worked in a pineapple processing plant
Jennifer Aniston was a waitress
Steven Spielberg whitewashed fruit trees

BEFORE THEY WERE PRESIDENTS...

Abraham Lincoln was a postmaster
Harry Truman was a railway timekeeper
Dwight Eisenhower was a football coach
Lyndon Johnson was a school principal
Jimmy Carter was a peanut farmer.

COLUMBUS

Doubt still hangs over the precise claim to fame of Columbus, the Italian explorer who encountered the Americas during three voyages at the end of the 15th century. Nevertheless, his name lives on in the US in numerous ways:

- *Columbus*, Capital of Ohio – there are also cities or towns named after him in Indiana, Georgia, Kansas, Mississippi, Nebraska, Wisconsin and Texas

- *Columbus County* – North Carolina

- *Columbus School of Law* – at the Catholic University of America in Washington, DC

- *Knights of Columbus* – Catholic men's fraternal benefit society

- *The Columbus Doors* – at the gateway to the Rotunda at the Capitol

- *Columbus Day* – declared a national holiday by President Franklin Roosevelt and celebrated on 12 October
- Sports teams that featured 'Columbus' in their name include the *Columbus Clippers*, the *Columbus Cottonmouths*, the *Columbus Wardogs* and the *Columbus Riverdragons*

FERTILE IMAGINATIONS

The combined harvester-thresher, which depended on pony power, was patented in America in 1836, and quickly became better known as a combine. The following year John Deere, an American blacksmith, invented the steel plough. The fertile lands of America could now be thoroughly exploited, and by the 1870s the combine – pulled by teams of 40 horses – was capable of cutting a width of around 10m (30ft).

ROYAL PREROGATIVE

In 1859, America had a self-declared emperor! Tired of governmental shortcomings, London-born Joshua Abraham Norton decided that a new no-nonsense rule was required – his own. He consequently declared himself as Imperial Highness Norton I, Emperor of the United States of America, and promptly abolished Congress. His local newspaper, the *San Francisco Bulletin*, published his proclamation on its front page.

The genial and flamboyant Norton made his astonishing bid for power after becoming bankrupt in 1856 and struggling to re-establish a business. Indulgent friends, who listened to his outbursts and even addressed him as 'Your Majesty', backed him. He proceeded to stride the streets of San Francisco in an officer's uniform with gold epaulettes and brass buttons, a black hat with a green feather, and a sabre hanging at his side. Norton survived by issuing tax demands to local shopkeepers and businesses, which were generally paid with good grace. He dined at local restaurants, yet was rarely presented with a bill. His correspondence went to heads of European states and he made earnest efforts to avert the American Civil War by mailing Lincoln and the Confederate chief Jefferson Davis. The emperor was one of the first people to observe the need for a suspension bridge spanning San Francisco Bay. When he died in the street in 1880, the city went into mourning. 'The King is Dead', announced newspaper headlines. More than 10,000 people filed past his coffin.

OSCAR FOR BEST ACTRESS

Date	Actress	Film
1928	Janet Gaynor	*7th Heaven, Street Angel* and *Sunrise*
1929	Mary Pickford	*Coquette*
1930	Norma Shearer	*The Divorcee*
1931	Marie Dressler	*Min And Bill*
1932	Helen Hayes	*The Sin Of Madelon Claudet*
1933	Katharine Hepburn	*Morning Glory*
1934	Claudette Colbert	*It Happened One Night*
1935	Bette Davis	*Dangerous*
1936	Luise Rainer	*The Great Ziegfeld*
1937	Luise Rainer	*The Good Earth*
1938	Bette Davis	*Jezebel*
1939	Vivien Leigh	*Gone With The Wind*
1940	Ginger Rogers	*Kitty Foyle*
1941	Joan Fontaine	*Suspicion*
1942	Greer Garson	*Mrs Miniver*
1943	Jennifer Jones	*The Song Of Bernadette*
1944	Ingrid Bergman	*Gaslight*
1945	Joan Crawford	*Mildred Pierce*
1946	Olivia De Havilland	*To Each His Own*
1947	Loretta Young	*The Farmer's Daughter*
1948	Jane Wyman	*Johnny Belinda*
1949	Olivia De Havilland	*The Heiress*
1950	Judy Holliday	*Born Yesterday*
1951	Vivien Leigh	*A Streetcar Named Desire*
1952	Shirley Booth	*Come Back, Little Sheba*
1953	Audrey Hepburn	*Roman Holiday*
1954	Grace Kelly	*The Country Girl*
1955	Anna Magnani	*The Rose Tattoo*
1956	Ingrid Bergman	*Anastasia*
1957	Joanne Woodward	*The Three Faces Of Eve*
1958	Susan Hayward	*I Want To Live!*
1959	Simone Signoret	*Room At The Top*
1960	Elizabeth Taylor	*Butterfield 8*
1961	Sophia Loren	*Two Women*
1962	Anne Bancroft	*The Miracle Worker*
1963	Patricia Neal	*Hud*
1964	Julie Andrews	*Mary Poppins*
1965	Julie Christie	*Darling*
1966	Elizabeth Taylor	*Who's Afraid Of Virginia Woolf?*

1967	Katharine Hepburn	*Guess Who's Coming To Dinner*
1968	Katharine Hepburn	*The Lion In Winter*
	Barbra Streisand	*Funny Girl*
1969	Maggie Smith	*The Prime Of Miss Jean Brodie*
1970	Glenda Jackson	*Women In Love*
1971	Jane Fonda	*Klute*
1972	Liza Minnelli	*Cabaret*
1973	Glenda Jackson	*A Touch Of Class*
1974	Ellen Burstyn	*Alice Doesn't Live Here Anymore*
1975	Louise Fletcher	*One Flew Over The Cuckoo's Nest*
1976	Faye Dunaway	*Network*
1977	Diane Keaton	*Annie Hall*
1978	Jane Fonda	*Coming Home*
1979	Sally Field	*Norma Rae*
1980	Sissy Spacek	*Coal Miner's Daughter*
1981	Katharine Hepburn	*On Golden Pond*
1982	Meryl Streep	*Sophie's Choice*
1983	Shirley Maclaine	*Terms Of Endearment*
1984	Sally Field	*Places In The Heart*
1985	Geraldine Page	*The Trip To Bountiful*
1986	Marlee Matlin	*Children Of A Lesser God*
1987	Cher	*Moonstruck*
1988	Jodie Foster	*The Accused*
1989	Jessica Tandy	*Driving Miss Daisy*
1990	Kathy Bates	*Misery*
1991	Jodie Foster	*The Silence Of The Lambs*
1992	Emma Thompson	*Howards End*
1993	Holly Hunter	*The Piano*
1994	Jessica Lange	*Blue Sky*
1995	Susan Sarandon	*Dead Man Walking*
1996	Frances McDormand	*Fargo*
1997	Helen Hunt	*As Good As It Gets*
1998	Gwyneth Paltrow	*Shakespeare In Love*
1999	Hilary Swank	*Boys Don't Cry*
2000	Julia Roberts	*Erin Brockovich*
2001	Halle Berry	*Monster's Ball*
2002	Nicole Kidman	*The Hours*

GUM TRADE

America's first vending machines appeared on New York City's railway station in 1888, and dispensed gum.

AMERICA'S MOST EMINENT ASSASSINATIONS

- John Wilkes Booth killed **Abraham Lincoln** at Ford Theater, Washington, on 14 April 1865, using a pistol.

- Charles J Guiteau, using a revolver, fatally injured US president **James A Garfield** at Baltimore & Potomac Railway Station, on 2 July 1881.

- **Jesse James** was killed by Bob Ford, using a pistol, in St Joseph, Missouri, on 3 April 1882.

- US president **William McKinley** died from wounds received at the Pan American Exposition, Buffalo, New York, on 6 September 1901. These were inflicted by Leon Czolgosz, with a pistol.

- Dr Carl Weiss, using a pistol, mortally wounded Senator **Huey Long** at Baton Rouge Capitol Building, Louisiana, on 8 September 1935.

- **John F Kennedy** died in Dallas, Texas, on 22 November 1963, after Lee Harvey Oswald apparently fired shots from a rifle.

- On 21 February 1965, black activist **Malcolm X** was shot by Thomas Hagan at a mosque in Harlem. Two other men were also jailed for the shooting.

- James Earl Ray used a rifle to kill civil rights campaigner **Martin Luther King** at Memphis, Tennessee, on 4 April 1968.

- **Robert Kennedy** died soon after being shot by Sirhan Sirhan at Los Angeles' Ambassador Hotel in the early hours of 5 June 1968.

- **John Lennon** died after being shot by Mark Chapman outside his New York apartment on 8 December 1980.

THE CAPITOL COMPLEX

The Capitol covers a ground area of about 1.6 hectares (4 acres), and has a floor area of nearly 7 hectares (16½ acres). Its length, from north to south, is 229m (751ft 4in), and its greatest width, including approaches, is 106.7m (350ft). Its height from the baseline on the east front to the top of the Statue of Freedom is 88m (288ft). From the basement floor to the top of the dome there is an ascent of 365 steps. The building contains approximately 540 rooms and has 658 windows (108 in the dome alone) and approximately 850 doorways. Each year, it is visited by between 3 million and 5 million people from around the world.

HEADLESS CHICKEN

When farmer Lloyd Olsen sized up a Wyandotte cockerel for dinner in September 1945, he aimed his axe high in order to accommodate his mother-in-law's taste for chicken neck. Having dealt the blow, the Colorado farmer was left speechless as the bird shook itself and continued to peck for grain, with no apparent regard for his lack of head. The following morning the cockerel, christened Mike, was still alive and Olsen set about feeding and watering it with an eye dropper into the severed neck.

As the bird began to thrive, Olsen transported the cockerel to the University of Utah in Salt Lake City, where it was discovered the blade had missed the jugular vein, a clot had formed to stop it bleeding to death, and that the brain stem was intact.

Olsen travelled the neighbourhood with his wonder bird, calling him 'a fine specimen of a chicken except for not having a head'. During the 18 months that remained of his life, Mike increased weight-wise from a paltry 1.1kg (2½lb) to 3.6kg (8lb). A 1.2m (4ft) metal sculpture formed out of farming implements including axe heads now stands in his home town, Fruita.

HEAVY HITTERS

Twelve of America's greatest heavyweight boxing champions are ranked below according to the number of bouts won. While few fight fans would deny Muhammad Ali his moniker of 'The Greatest', it's worth noting that Rocky Marciano defeated all 49 opponents in his nine-year career. He remains the only undefeated world heavyweight champion in boxing history.

Name	Professional career	Record (won–lost–drawn)
George Foreman	1969–97	76–5–0
Earnie Shavers	1969–95	73–14–1
Larry Holmes	1973–2002	69–6–0
Joe Louis	1934–51	68–3–0
Jack Dempsey	1914–27	61–6–8
Muhammad Ali	1960–81	56–5–0
Floyd Patterson	1952–72	55–8–1
Sonny Liston	1953–70	50–4–0
Rocky Marciano	1947–55	49–0–0
Riddick Bowe	1989–96	40–1–0
James Buster Douglas	1981–99	38–6–1
Joe Frazier	1965–81	32–4–1

AMERICAN HERO

When General MacArthur returned to America in April 1951 after being fired by President Harry Truman, it was the first time he had been home since before the start of World War II. MacArthur had been in charge of American forces in the southwest Pacific after Pearl Harbour, and then he supervised the occupation of vanquished Japan. By 1951, he was in command in Korea – until comments he made about American policy in the region riled Truman and also fellow army officers. On his return, the immensely popular commander received a rapturous welcome, with an estimated seven million people turning out to flag up their support for him.

However, public sympathy soon waned when it became clear his personal preference was for war with China. Later, President Truman said, 'I fired him because he wouldn't respect the authority of the President. I didn't fire him because he was a dumb son-of-a-bitch, although he was, but that's not against the law for generals.'

PRESIDENTIAL STAR SIGNS

As everyone knows, America still awaits its first female president and a ground-breaking black president. However, it is a lesser known fact that no one born under the star sign Gemini (21 May–21 June) has yet moved into the White House to have a finger poised on the nuclear trigger. As Geminian traits include a restless nature and an impractical outlook, perhaps this is no bad thing. Presidential birth signs, with their chief characteristics, are as follows:

Aries (born leader, energetic, intolerant)
Thomas Jefferson
John Tyler

Taurus (Stable, thorough, dull)
James Monroe
James Buchanan
Ulysses Grant
Harry Truman

Cancer (Shrewd, loyal, introspective)
John Quincy Adams
Calvin Coolidge
Gerald Ford
George W Bush

Leo (Open, courageous, cold-hearted)
Benjamin Harrison
Herbert Hoover
John F Kennedy
Geogre HW Bush
Bill Clinton

Virgo (Sympathetic, dedicated, critical)
William Taft
Lyndon Johnson

Libra (Sincere, broad-minded, domineering)
Rutherford Hayes
Chester Arthur
Dwight Eisenhower
Jimmy Carter

Scorpio (Protective, dynamic, secretive)
John Adams
James Polk
James Garfield
Theodore Roosevelt
Warren Harding

Sagittarius (Honest, straightforward, philosophical)
Martin Van Buren
Zachary Taylor
Franklin Pierce

Capricorn (Optimistic, enthusiastic, hot-headed)
Millard Fillmore
Andrew Johnson
Woodrow Wilson
Richard Nixon

Aquarius (Inventive, caring, self-centered)
William Harrison
Abraham Lincoln
William McKinley
Franklin Roosevelt
Ronald Reagan

Pisces (Compassionate, hard-working, self-pitying)
Geogre Washington
James Madison
Andrew Jackson
Grover Cleveland

PAMMY'S LEGAL WHAMMY

Buxom *Baywatch* actress Pamela Anderson reckons to have spent at least half her lifetime earnings on legal action to recover the rights to her name. The problem arose in the early days of the World Wide Web when she discovered it had been unwittingly sold off.

Given that the search engine Google logs around 180 million searches *per day* for Pamela Anderson – mostly from porn site seekers – her total losses may approach billions of dollars. 'Ultimately,' she says, 'my opponents couldn't prove they had something that was more Pamela Anderson than me.' Must have been a great case to try!

BIG BIRD FLIES BIG APPLE

Concorde – flight BA002 – took off for the last time from JFK airport on the afternoon of 24 October 2003, ending a 26-year history of commercial supersonic travel between London and New York. With no obvious successor in sight it seems the aircraft will hold its transatlantic speed record for passenger services (an impressive two hours recorded on 7 February 1996) for some time yet.

ICE TO BE GAY

The first openly gay Anglican bishop, Gene Robinson of New Hampshire, was consecrated at an ice hockey arena in Durham, NH, on Sunday 2 November 2003.

CANCER SCARE

According to the American Cancer Society, 556,500 Americans were expected to die from cancer in the year 2003 – that's 1,500 people a day. Cancer is the second leading cause of death in the US, the first being heart disease. One in four deaths that occur in the country are due to cancer.

US PORTS AND HARBOURS

Anchorage, Baltimore, Boston, Charleston, Chicago, Duluth, Hampton Roads, Honolulu, Houston, Jacksonville, Los Angeles, New Orleans, New York, Philadelphia, Port Canaveral, Portland (Oregon), Prudhoe Bay, San Francisco, Savannah, Seattle, Tampa, Toledo.

A QUESTION OF FAITH

Religious movements that began in the US, with the names of the accredited founders in brackets:

The Church of Jesus Christ of Latter-Day Saints (Mormons) (Joseph Smith, 1805–44)

Christian Science (Mary Baker Eddy, 1821–1910)

Scientology (Lafayette Ron Hubbard, 1911–86)

Jehovah's Witness (Charles Taze Russell, 1852–1916)

The Children of God (David Berg, 1919–94)

Eckankar (Paul Twitchell, 1908–71)

Moral Re-Armament (Frank ND Buchman, 1878–1961)

FBI BUDGET FOR 2003

In fiscal year 2003, the FBI received a total of $4.298 billion (£2.541 billion), including $540.281 million (£320 million) in net program increases to enhance counterterrorism, counterintelligence, cybercrime, information technology, security, forensics, training and criminal programs.

HORROR AT GREEN RIVER

Truck painter Gary Ridgway has more murders on his court record than any other US serial killer. At his Seattle trial in November 2003, the 54-year-old from Auburn, Washington, admitted to 48 of the 'Green River killings', so-called because they occurred near the river running through his home state.

Most of Ridgway's victims were female prostitutes or runaways. 'I hate most prostitutes and I did not want to pay them for sex,' he told police. 'I thought I could kill as many of them as I wanted without getting caught.' Most of his victims were strangled and mutilated after death.

Incredibly, Ridgway escaped the death penalty under a plea-bargaining deal. He was given 48 consecutive life sentences and warned that he would never be freed.

It is thought America's worst serial killers were Henry Lee Lucas and Ottis Toole who, detectives believe, murdered more than 200 people during the 1970s and 1980s in the Deep South. There wasn't enough proof to link them to all the deaths.

FBI'S TEN MOST WANTED

In March 1950 J Edgar Hoover launched the FBI's Ten Most Wanted list. At the close of 2003 the list was as follows:

Michael Alfonso
Born: 26 June 1969
Nationality: American
Reward for information: $50,000 (£30,000)

A registered sex offender, Alfonso is wanted for allegedly stalking and shooting two former girlfriends in Illinois.

Osama Bin Laden
Born: 1957
Nationality: Saudi Arabian
Reward for information: $25 million (£14.8 million) plus a further $2 million (£1.2 million) through a program funded by the Airline Pilots' Association.

Bin Laden is wanted in connection with the bombings of the US embassies in Dar Es Salaam and Nairobi in August 1998, and the World Trade Center and Pentagon in 2001.

Hopeton Eric Brown
Born: 26 September 1974
Nationality: Jamaican
Reward for information: up to $50,000 (£30,000)

In America, Brown is being sought for his alleged drug-related activities and murder. In Jamaica, the police want to question him about two murders in Montego Bay.

James J Bulger
Born: 3 September 1929
Nationality: American
Reward for information: up to $1 million (£600,000)

Bulger is suspected of involvement in gangland murders during a decade in the Boston area.

Genero Espinso Dorantes
Born: 19 June 1970
Nationality: Mexican
Reward for information: up to $50,000 (£30,000)

Dorantes is wanted for allegedly torturing and murdering his four-year-old stepson in Nashville, Tennessee, in February 2003. He is thought to be involved in transporting illegal aliens from Mexico to America.

Victor Manuel Gerena

Born: 24 June 1958
Nationality: American
Reward for information: up to $50,000 (£30,000)

Gerena is being sought in connection with an armed raid in which two security guards were held at hostage before $7 million (£4 million) was stolen.

Glen Stewart Godwin

Born: 26 June 1958
Nationality: American
Reward for information: up to $50,000 (£30,000)

Having twice escaped from behind bars where he was serving sentences for (different) murders, Godwin is thought to be involved with drugs trafficking.

Richard Steve Goldberg

Born: 9 November 1945
Nationality: American
Reward for information: up to $50,000 (£30,000)

Goldberg is wanted for allegedly engaging in sexual activities with girls under the age of ten in Long Beach, California.

Donald Eugene Webb

Born: 14 July 1931
Nationality: American
Reward for information: up to $50,000 (£30,000)

Webb is wanted in connection with the brutal murder of a police chief in Pennsylvania.

Robert William Fisher

Born: 13 April 1961
Nationality: American
Reward for information: up to $50,000 (£30,000)

Fisher is wanted for allegedly killing his wife and two young children in Scottsdale, Arizona, in 2001, before blowing up the family home.

PRIORITIES OF THE FEDERAL BUREAU OF INVESTIGATION (FBI)

- Protect the United States from terrorist attack
- Protect the United States against foreign intelligence operations and espionage
- Protect the United States against cyber-based attacks and high-technology crimes
- Combat public corruption at all levels
- Protect civil rights
- Combat transnational and national criminal organisations and enterprises
- Combat major white-collar crime
- Combat significant violent crime
- Support federal, state, county, municipal, and international partners
- Upgrade technology to successfully perform the FBI's mission
  The FBI motto is 'Fidelity, Bravery and Integrity'.

PRESIDENTIAL PETS

The vast majority of American presidents have had pet pooches, feline friends and even a horse or two. A few, however, were notably animal crackers and stocked the White House (and other addresses) with creatures great and small. Here are the six most ardent animal lovers ever to sit in the Oval Office, together with a list of their pets.

Abraham Lincoln: He owned Jack the turkey, goats named Nanny and Nanko, ponies, pigs, a white rabbit and assorted cats and dogs.

Ulysses Grant: In his menageries there was a Newfoundland dog called Faithful, eight horses, ponies called Reb and Billy Buttons, pigs, dogs, roosters and a parrot.

Theodore Roosevelt: In addition to a selection of dogs and cats, Teddy Roosevelt kept a badger called Josiah, Algonquin the pony, Eli the piebald rat, Emily Spinach the snake, five bears, five guinea pigs, two kangaroo rats, lizards, roosters, an owl, a flying squirrel, a coyote, a lion, a hyena, a zebra and horses.

Calvin Coolidge: Among the more unusual animals kept by Coolidge were two raccoons called Rebecca and Horace, Ebeneezer the donkey, Smokey, a bobcat, Old Bill the thrush, a goose called Enoch, a mockingbird, a bear, an antelope, a wallaby, a pygmy hippo and some lion cubs.

John F Kennedy: In the Kennedy household the pets included Robin the canary, Zsa Zsa the rabbit, parakeets Bluebell and Marybelle, hamsters Debbie and Bill as well as a horse, ponies, dogs and Tom Kitten the cat.

Lyndon Johnson: Dog-lover Johnson also found room for hamsters and lovebirds.

FEDERAL BUREAU OF PRISONS FACTS

Institutions: 103

Total inmate population: 171,562

Inmates by gender:
Male: 159,782 (93.1%)
Female: 11,780 (6.9%)

Inmates by race:
White: 96,761 (56.4%)
Black: 69,311 (40.4%)
Asian: 2,745 (1.6%)
Native American: 2,745 (1.6%)

Average Age of Inmate: 37 years

Types of offences
Drug offences: 85,209 (54.8%)
Weapons, explosives, arson: 17,311 (11.2%)
Immigration: 16,369 (10.5%)
Robbery: 10,284 (6.6%)
Burglary, larceny, property offences: 7,138 (4.6%)
Extortion, fraud, bribery: 7,046 (4.5%)
Homicide, aggravated assault and kidnapping offences: 5,170 (3.3%)
Miscellaneous: 2,845 (1.8%)
Sex offences: 1,584 (1.0%)
Banking and insurance, counterfeit, embezzlement: 1,046 (0.7%)
Courts or corrections (eg obstructing justice): 743 (0.5%)
Continuing criminal enterprise: 628 (0.4%)
National security: 89 (0.1%)

STRIKING LUCKY

In 1942 cigarette manufacturers Lucky Strike abandoned its familiar company colours for the sake of the war effort which apparently required the titanium in green ink. The Lucky Strike packet was left white save for a single red bull's eye. In response to its patriotism, sales rose by 38 per cent.

PEARLS OF WISDOM

Mark Twain, (1835–1910) US novelist

'All you need in this life is ignorance and confidence, and then success is sure.'

'Name the greatest of all the inventors. Accident.'

'It was wonderful to find America, but it would have been still more wonderful to miss it.'

'Many a small thing has been made large by the right kind of advertising.'

'Only kings, editors and people with tapeworm have the right to use the editorial "we".'

'If you pick up a starving dog and make him prosperous, he will not bite you. This is the principal difference between a dog and a man.'

'A lie can travel half way around the world while the truth is putting on its shoes.'

'Denial ain't just a river in Egypt.'

Groucho Marx, (1890–1977) US comedian

'I find television very educational. Every time someone switches it on I go into another room and read a good book.'

'I eat like a vulture. Unfortunately the resemblance doesn't end there.'

'Politics is the art of looking for trouble, finding it, misdiagnosing it and then misapplying the wrong remedies.'

'I never forget a face, but I'll make an exception in your case.'

'Military intelligence is a contradiction in terms.'

Truman Capote, (1924–84) US novelist

'It's a scientific fact that if you stay in California, you lose one point of IQ every year.'

'Life is a moderately good play with a badly written third act.'

'Failure is the condiment that gives success its flavor.'

'I don't care what anybody says about me as long as it isn't true.'

Samuel Goldwyn, (1882–1974) movie mogul

'Television has raised writing to a new low.'

'Let's have some new cliches.'

'An oral contract isn't worth the paper it's written on.'

'Anyone who goes to a psychiatrist ought to have his head examined.'

'I want you to put more life into your dying.'

Abraham Lincoln, (1809–65) US President

'Those who deny freedom to others, deserve it not for themselves; and, under a just God, can not long retain it.'

'As I would not be a slave, so I would not be a master. Whatever differs from this, to the extent of the difference, is no democracy.'

'Let us have faith that right makes might, and in that faith, let us, to the end, dare to do our duty as we understand it.'

'I leave you, hoping that the lamp of liberty will burn in your bosoms until there shall no longer be a doubt that all men are created free and equal.'

'Common looking people are the best in the world: that is the reason the Lord makes so many of them.'

INDEX

Everything You Didn't Need To Know About The UK

Nick Brownlee

EVERYTHING YOU DIDN'T NEED TO KNOW ABOUT THE UK

Nick Brownlee

How did Big Ben get its name? Why do 51 per cent of Brits sleep naked? Was the Queen really sending emails in the 1970s? And just how do you make the perfect cup of tea?

Packed with inane anecdotes and useless trivia, *Everything You didn't Need To Know About The UK* is a compilation of weird and intriguing facts concerning all things British and the ultimate guide to understanding the minutiae of life in the Mother Country.

UK | 1-86074-562-8 | £9.99
US | 1-86074-597-0 | $13.95

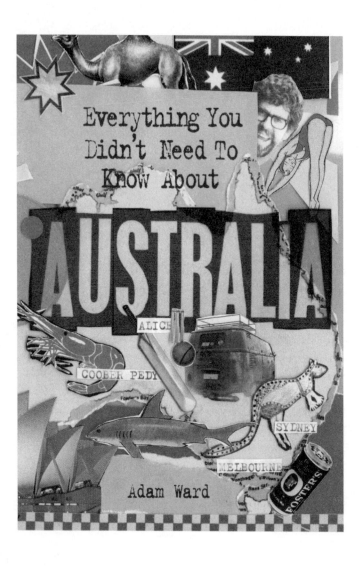

EVERYTHING YOU DIDN'T NEED TO KNOW ABOUT AUSTRALIA
Adam Ward

What are the dining rituals of the Tasmanian Devil? Which soap stars did manage to make it behind the microphone? How was the boomerang used as a musical instrument by the Aborigones? And just what do the Aussies think can be fixed with wire and pantyhose?

Packed with inane anecdotes and useless trivia, *Everything You didn't Need To Know About Australia* is a compilation of weird and intriguing facts concerning all things Antipodean and the ultimate guide to understanding the minutiae of life down under.

UK | 1-86074-561-X | £9.99
US | 1-86074-598-9 | $13.95